To Hunt, To Shoot, To Entertain:
Clericalism and the Catholic Laity

RUSSELL SHAW

To Hunt, To Shoot, To Entertain: Clericalism and the Catholic Laity

WIPF & STOCK · Eugene, Oregon

Wipf and Stock Publishers
199 W 8th Ave, Suite 3
Eugene, OR 97401

To Hunt, To Shoot, To Entertain
Clericalism and the Catholic Laity
By Shaw, Russell
Copyright©1993 by Shaw, Russell
ISBN 13: 978-1-61097-203-1
Publication date 8/1/2011
Previously published by Ignatius Press, 1993

CONTENTS

Acknowledgments	7
I. An Overview of Clericalism	9
II. A Brief History of Clericalism	39
III. Vatican II and After	83
IV. Problems of the Present Moment	111
V. From Power to Vocation	143
VI. Beyond Clericalism	173

ACKNOWLEDGMENTS

It will be apparent from the text that I am deeply indebted to Dr. Germain Grisez for many of the fundamental ideas that underlie this study. Less obvious, except in the results, are the innumerable practical criticisms that he offered for the book's improvement. I also owe a particular debt of gratitude to Mr. Carl Schmitt for his thoughtful reactions at several stages and especially for his suggestions regarding the second chapter.

In addition, I wish to express my gratitude for ideas and support of various kinds to the following: Dennis Bartlett, Dennis Bolster, David Byers, Rev. Robert Connor, John Crosby, Richard Doerflinger, Dwight Duncan, Robert Jackson, Rev. Msgr. George Kelly, Philip Lawler, Rev. Msgr. Richard Malone, William E. May, and Patrick Riley. If I have forgotten any, it is not for lack of appreciation of their kindness and generosity.

The translation of Scripture used here (except for Scripture passages embedded in other texts) is the Revised Standard Version, Catholic edition. The translation of the documents of the Second Vatican Council is *The Documents of Vatican II*, Walter M. Abbott, S.J., and Joseph Gallagher, eds. (New York: Guild Press, 1966).

I

AN OVERVIEW OF CLERICALISM

"Really," said the priest, a friend of mine, when I told him I was writing a book about clericalism, "I don't think it's much of a problem. There is a lot of *anti*clericalism out there among feminists over the women's ordination thing. But you don't find much clericalism any more."

I think that is wrong, for three reasons.

First, even though generous, large-minded priests no longer consciously espouse clerical elitism, the attitudes and assumptions of the clericalist mentality, often unrecognized as such, still find expression among clerics in a number of ways, some of them surprising.

Second, old-fashioned clericalism dominates the thinking and behavior of large numbers of Catholic laymen. The Catholic laity may now be more clericalized than their clergy.

Third, by a kind of dialectical process, the distorted views of the Church, clerics, and laymen that helped spawn the classic clericalism of the past are today giving rise to another set of confusions about priesthood and the lay condition that are the mirror image of clerical elitism.

Much of this book will be devoted to explaining these three statements. But at the outset we need to consider a basic question: What is clericalism? Rather than begin with a textbook definition, let us consider some instances of clericalism at work.

In April 1867, a British Catholic journal called the *Weekly Register* reported that Pope Pius IX had decided against allowing John Henry Newman to lead a Catholic return to Oxford. Considering the sensitivity of the assignment, the *Register*'s Rome correspondent wrote, "Only an Ultramontane without a taint in his fidelity" could be trusted.[1] This slur on Newman's loyalty produced dramatic results, among them an open letter addressed to Newman and signed by two hundred leading British lay Catholics, including all the Catholic members of Parliament, nearly all the Catholic peers, and other prominent persons. "We feel that every blow that touches you inflicts a wound upon the Catholic Church in this country", they told the distinguished convert.[2]

Gratifying as this may have been to Newman and his friends, not everyone was well pleased. Among the most displeased was Monsignor George Talbot, the British ultramontanists' man in Rome. He wrote Archbishop Henry Edward Manning of Westminster, bitterly assailing Newman and his lay supporters. Citing other recent incidents, Talbot warned that "if a check be not placed on the laity of England they will be the rulers of the Catholic Church in England instead of the Holy See and the Episcopate." Laymen, he said, "are beginning to show the cloven hoof". After more of the same, he delivered his rhetorical *coup de grace:*

"What is the province of the laity? To hunt, to shoot, to entertain? These matters they understand, but to meddle with ecclesiastical matters they have no right at all, and this affair of Newman is a matter purely ecclesiastical. . . . Dr. Newman is the most dangerous man in England, and you will see that he will make use of the laity against your Grace."[3]

---

[1] See Ian Ker, *John Henry Newman* (Oxford: Oxford University Press, 1990), 603; Robert Gray, *Cardinal Manning* (New York: St. Martin's Press, 1985), 214.

[2] Ker, 605.

[3] Quoted in John Coulson, Introduction, in John Henry Newman, *On Consulting the Faithful in Matters of Doctrine* (New York: Sheed & Ward, 1961), 41–42.

A long history, important to our subject, lies behind this outburst. It is convenient to begin the story in 1859.

In its issues of January and February of that year a lay-edited British Catholic journal called the *Rambler* published two articles arguing for Catholic cooperation with a royal commission set up to investigate the state of elementary education. Alas, the British bishops, fearing government interference in religious education, earlier had reached the opposite conclusion: Catholics should *not* cooperate.

This was not the first time the *Rambler* and its lay editors had crossed swords with the bishops. The new confrontation led rapidly to a shakeup of the review's editorial staff and to the suggestion that Dr. Newman, apparently deemed acceptable to all parties, take charge. He agreed in March, with the first issue under his direction appearing in May.[4]

It contained an unsigned editorial about the bishops and the royal commission. Wrote the new editor, "We do unfeignedly believe . . . that their Lordships really desire to know the opinions of the laity on subjects in which the laity are especially concerned. If even in the preparation of a dogmatic definition the faithful are consulted, as lately in the instance of the Immaculate Conception, it is at least as natural to anticipate such an act of kind feeling and sympathy in great practical questions."

Kind feeling and sympathy aside, the upshot of this sally was that on May 22 Newman found himself in an interview with his ordinary, the friendly Bishop Ullathorne of Birmingham. Newman reported the conversation this way: "He said something like 'Who are the laity?' I answered (not these words) that the Church would look foolish without them." On Ullathorne's suggestion, Newman resigned as editor of the *Rambler*.

The July issue, the last under Newman's direction, featured a long article entitled "On Consulting the Faithful in Matters of Doctrine". It proved to be a bombshell that led to New-

---

[4] For an account of these events, see Coulson, 1–49.

man's delation to Rome and cast a cloud over his reputation for many years after, as the events of 1867 were so dramatically to show.

The argument of "On Consulting the Faithful" is that the bishops do well to ascertain the views of laymen not only about practical matters but also, as Newman had written in the *Rambler* in May, about doctrinal ones. That is because "the body of the faithful is one of the witnesses to the fact of the tradition of revealed doctrine, and because their *consensus* through Christendom is the voice of the Infallible Church".[5] Not that this lay consensus is itself infallible, but, where it truly exists, it points to the infallible faith of the Church as a whole.[6]

The author uses the history of the Arian heresy in the fourth century to illustrate his point. In face of this challenge, laymen by and large remained faithful to orthodox belief in the divinity of Christ, but many bishops went over to the heretics' camp. Newman's way of expressing this is not unprovocative: "The body of the episcopate was unfaithful to its commission, while the body of the laity was faithful to its baptism."[7]

After quoting a vivid contemporary account of the rejoicing with which the laity greeted the Council of Ephesus' declaration that the Virgin Mary was truly Mother of God, Newman ends with a justly famous observation of his own: "I think certainly that the *Ecclesia docens* is more happy when she has such enthusiastic partisans about her as are here represented, than when she cuts off the faithful from the study of her divine doctrines and the sympathy of her divine contemplations, and requires from them a *fides implicita* in her word, which in the educated classes will terminate in indifference, and in the poorer in superstition."[8]

---

[5] Newman, 63.
[6] See Vatican Council II, *Lumen Gentium*, 12.
[7] Newman, 76.
[8] Ibid., 106.

Clericalism goes back far beyond the middle years of the nineteenth century, however, back even to the Church's very beginnings. Clericalism is *not* ultramontanism, *not* failure to consult the laity; it is something deeper and more pervasive.

Jesus was a victim of the clericalist mentality of his time and place. Having challenged the authority of the religious and social elite of a theocratic society, he paid with his life. His prosecution and death at his enemies' hands conform to a pattern to which he earlier called attention: "Woe to you, scribes and Pharisees, hypocrites! . . . I send you prophets and wise men and scribes, some of whom you will kill and crucify, and some you will scourge in your synagogues and persecute from town to town."[9]

In the Catholic Church today, of course, clericalism is not literally responsible for anybody's death. Although its victims are very numerous, they suffer mainly a psychological and spiritual martyrdom of which, very often, they are not even themselves fully aware. Yet the clericalist mind-set does fundamentally distort, disrupt, and poison the Christian lives of members of the Church, clergy and laity alike, and weakens the Church in her mission of service to the world. Clericalism is not the cause of every problem of the Church, but it causes many and is a factor in many more. Time and again, as we shall see, it plays a role in the debilitating controversies that today afflict the Catholic community in the United States and other countries.

Clericalism assumes that clerics not only are but also are *meant* to be the active, dominant elite in the Church, and laymen the passive, subservient mass. As a result, the laity are discouraged from taking seriously their responsibility for the Church's mission, and evangelization is neglected. So are efforts to influence the structures of secular society on behalf of the values of the gospel—the evangelization of culture, as it is called. A large part of the program of the Second

---

[9] Mt 23:29, 34.

Vatican Council remains not only unaccomplished but also unattempted.

Clericalism deepens the confusion about lay and clerical identity and roles that is a factor in the morale problems apparently troubling some priests. In this way it also deepens the so-called vocations crisis in the Church in this and other Western countries. Although the clericalist mentality typically defines this crisis as a shortfall of new candidates for the priesthood and religious life, the crisis of vocations in its entirety also includes the apparent failure of many laymen not only to discern their vocations but even to give serious thought to the question of vocation. Clericalism likewise is a factor in the inappropriate political activism of some clerics, and it plays a role in the controversy over women's ordination. We shall consider all these matters below.

Perhaps most serious of all, clericalism tends to discourage laymen from cultivating a spirituality that rises above a rather low level of fervor and intensity. As the clericalist mentality sees it, the serious pursuit of sanctity is the business of priests and religious. For the laity, Vatican II's universal call to holiness remains a muted trumpet. Minimalistic religious practice and legalistic morality are all that are asked of laymen and all many ask of themselves, while the idea that they should aspire to sanctity is dismissed as spiritual pretentiousness—"salvation in the fast lane".[10]

We need to be aware, though, not just of the harm done directly and visibly by the mentality of clerical elitism but also of the destructive operation of a kind of clericalist dialectic. This process has produced a number of troublesome offspring in reaction to the original abuse.

History is instructive on this point. The clericalist mentality in its political guise—a form of overreaching that usurped the role of the laity in the political order—helps account for the rise of European anticlericalism in the eighteenth and

---

[10] Clifford Longley, book review in *The Tablet*, May 27, 1989.

nineteenth centuries. That is hardly surprising, since, as Yves Congar remarks, "forgetfulness of the true role of lay people leads both to clericalism in the Church and to laicism in the world".[11] This laicism has been marked by its fierce determination to exclude religious influence from public life and, in its most virulent forms, by overt or covert persecution of religion. Its malign influence continues to be felt in the United States even today: for example, in certain absolutist ways of thinking about church-state separation and as an element in the mind-set of secular humanism.

Within the Church, the dialectic of clericalism now generates still other bad results. Notable among these is an exaggerated interest on the part of some laity and clergy in power-sharing arrangements based on the assumption that the advancement of laymen requires admitting them to offices and functions previously reserved for clerics—allowing them to look and act like priests. Lay ministries, for all that can and should be said in their favor, sometimes reflect this way of thinking.

The underlying problem expresses itself in many ways and contexts. Consider the findings of a survey asking Catholics which option they would prefer in the face of a shortage of priests, the recruitment of more clergy or "think[ing] of new ways to structure parish leadership to include more deacons, sisters and lay persons".[12] Older Catholics generally preferred the first approach; younger Catholics, the second.

The trouble with this Hobson's choice is not that the alternatives are, exactly, wrong but that they do not reach the heart of the problem and its solution. When finding people for ministry is reduced to the either/or of clerical recruitment on the one hand and structural tinkering on the other, one is entitled to respond, "As a long-term response—neither, thank you." I hope to show at length before I am done that the long-term solution to this problem requires that every

[11] Yves Congar, *Lay People in the Church* (London: Geoffrey Chapman, 1985), 53.
[12] John A. Coleman, S. J., "Young Adults: A Look at the Demographics", *Commonweal*, Sept. 14, 1990.

member of the Church realize that he has a vocation and engage in discernment to learn what it is.

Today, too, the clericalist dialectic gives rise to a kind of neocongregationalism, expressed in the writings of some theologians and theological popularizers and apparently acted out here and there by people who see themselves as an avant-garde underground Church.[13] Like many other exaggerations, neocongregationalism starts from an important truth: the common priesthood of the faithful. Long neglected in Catholic thought and practice, this ancient doctrine has come to the fore in the years since Vatican Council II, but at a price—the confusions embodied in neocongregationalism.

There is a strong draught of it in the account provided by a Canadian theologian, Remi Parent. Observing that the baptismal condition "constitutes *an unsurpassable horizon of life, of intelligibility, and of action*", he asserts, "Nothing, absolutely nothing, can be experienced, understood, or done that can be situated *above* or *beside* the baptismal priesthood."[14] On this basis he draws the following conclusion: "[T]he presbyteral and episcopal service is not humanly viable unless, by rediscovering the unicity of the priesthood of Christ, one recognizes a single historical participation in this priesthood, that which constitutes precisely the *baptismal priesthood*. . . . [T]*here cannot be in history any other Christian priesthood than the baptismal priesthood.*"[15]

Does this dictum apply to the Eucharist? In fact, Parent argues, especially there: "Christians must . . . rediscover that the eucharist does not exist for them if they do not take the

---

[13] A recent survey of the theological literature: Patrick J. Dunn, *Priesthood: A Re-examination of the Roman Catholic Theology of the Presbyterate* (Staten Island, N.Y.: Alba House, 1990), 19–44.

[14] Remi Parent, *A Church of the Baptized: Overcoming the Tension between the Clergy and the Laity* (Mahwah, N.J.: Paulist Press, 1989), 76–77; italics in original.

[15] Ibid., 99, 101.

(always historical) responsibility of making it exist." And, lest there be any doubt about what that means: "Is this to say that the clerics lose all place at the mass? One thing is certain: they will lose it if they do not cease to be and to behave like clerics. . . . Furthermore, they have in fact already lost their old place where certain persons and communities have begun to forsake the schemas of the magical mentality"[16] — in other words, where nonordained persons attempt to celebrate the Eucharist in the absence of an ordained priest.

It hardly needs saying that this way of thinking marks a radical departure from the teaching of Vatican II that the common priesthood and the ministerial or hierarchical priesthood "differ from one another in essence and not only in degree".[17] And Vatican II's teaching on this matter is, of course, by no means new; it restates a truth of Catholic Faith already definitively taught by the Council of Trent.[18]

While Vatican II does not go into detail about the nature of the difference between ordained and nonordained, there have been helpful efforts to clarify it in the years since then. An important paper published in 1970 by the International Theological Commission identifies the distinctiveness of the ordained priesthood this way: "[T]he Christian who is called to the priestly ministry receives by his ordination not a merely external function but a new sharing in the priesthood of Christ, by virtue of which he represents Christ at the head of the community and, as it were, facing the community. The ministry is therefore a specific way of exercising the Christian service in the Church. This specific character is seen especially in the priest's role of presiding at the Eucharist, a role that is necessary for the full realization of the Christian worship."[19]

---

[16] Ibid., 124–25.

[17] *Lumen Gentium*, 10.

[18] DS 1771–78.

[19] "The Priestly Ministry", in Michael Sharkey, ed., *International Theological Commission: Texts and Documents, 1969–1985* (San Francisco: Ignatius Press, 1989), 87.

Later, in pursuing this question, we shall follow up these themes.

It is my intention, however, not to enter into a debate with Catholic neocongregationalism but only to take note of it as a byproduct of the clericalist dialectic. Although its exaggerated emphasis upon baptismal priesthood is sometimes depicted as a healthy reaction against clericalism, it actually is a mirror image of clericalist values that arises from essentially the same sources: deep-seated confusion on the subject of vocation, pervasive depreciation of the secular order and the laity's duties there, and an implicit conviction that, for laymen *really* to enjoy dignity in the Church, they must become and begin to do exactly what the ordained clergy are and do. (That is to say, the progress of the laity requires that they be clericalized.)

In the final analysis, as neocongregationalism sees things, an autonomous baptismal ministry carried on by Christians in and to the world does not count for much after all. What matters is the familiar clericalist model of Christian life, with its stress on roles and functions within the safe structures of the ecclesiastical institution.

The shortage of priests and of new priestly vocations in the United States and other Western countries makes it likely that many of the problems under examination here will grow worse in the years just ahead. No longer, it seems, can the brittle carapace of clericalism shield the priesthood against a hostile culture; and as the priesthood suffers, so does the rest of the Church.

According to one study, the number of active diocesan priests in the United States is on its way to a 40 percent drop over a forty-year span—from thirty-five thousand in 1966 to twenty-one thousand by 2005. The situation is said to be much the same for religious order priests—a 35 percent decline from about twenty thousand in 1975 to thirteen thousand in 2005.[20] For our purposes it makes little difference whether these figures somewhat overestimate or underestimate the decline or get it exactly right. A serious shortage of pastoral care already exists in some places in this country, and it is sure to grow worse in the years ahead. Priestless parishes and priestless Sundays are now part of the reality of Catholic America. We shall see much more of them.

As long as clericalist ways of thinking persist, we also are likely to find that efforts to deal with the shortage of priests by multiplying lay ministers—something that arguably should and must be done—will heighten the confusion that already exists concerning lay and clerical roles and identities. We are likely to find more credence given—out of desperation, if for no other reason—to the leveling proposal of neocongregationalism.[21] As these trends feed off and reinforce one another, we may even find the shortage of priests and priestly vocations becoming worse than current projections suggest.

These things need not happen. Clericalism increases the chances that they will.

Still, it would be wrong to speak only of problems and dangers, as if nothing good had happened since Vatican II with respect to the position of laymen in the Church and their relationship to the clergy.

Not even in the past did clericalism keep either the laity or priests from living wholesome, productive lives, achieving personal holiness, and serving the Church and the world in a multitude of ways. During the past three decades Vatican II and postconciliar developments like the revised Code of Canon Law published in 1983, the 1987 Synod of Bishops

[20] See Richard A. Schoenherr and Lawrence A. Young, *The Catholic Priest in the U.S.: Demographic Investigations* (Madison, Wis.: Comparative Religious Organization Studies Publications, 1990).

[21] See, e.g., Bernard Cooke, "Entire Faith Community Performs Eucharist", *National Catholic Reporter*, May 18, 1990.

on the Laity, and Pope John Paul II's postsynodal apostolic exhortation *Christifideles Laici* ("On the Vocation and the Mission of the Lay Faithful in the Church and in the World") have broken new ground in thinking and practice concerning laymen. One purpose of this book is to call attention to the breakthroughs, so that they will consciously be used as the basis for further progress in the future.

Pope John Paul gives a positive summary of what has been happening in these years: "[T]he new manner of active collaboration among priests, religious and the lay faithful; the active participation in the Liturgy, in the proclamation of the Word of God and catechesis; the multiplicity of services and tasks entrusted to the lay faithful and fulfilled by them; the flourishing of groups, associations, and spiritual movements as well as a lay commitment in the life of the Church; and . . . the fuller and meaningful participation of women in the development of society."[22]

Noteworthy, too, has been the rise of the lay "groups, associations, and spiritual movements" upon which Pope John Paul remarks. As Hans Urs von Balthasar points out, these truly are something new under the sun: "Not until our own century do we see the spread of such a flourishing variety of self-sufficient lay movements in the Church."[23]

Even so, the persistence of old-fashioned clericalism and the emergence, through a dialectical process, of recent byproducts of the clericalist mentality underline the presence, in the Catholic psyche as well as in the structures of the Church, of some deep-rooted, largely unrecognized problem or cluster of problems. If abuses like these continue to flourish despite so much manifest goodwill and intelligence, they must have their source in a fundamental error of concept or structure.

---

[22] *Christifideles Laici*, 2.

[23] Hans Urs von Balthasar, 1982 position paper for the Pontifical Council for the Laity, quoted in Paul Josef Cordes, *In the Midst of Our World: Forces of Spiritual Renewal* (San Francisco: Ignatius Press, 1988), 22.

We need to probe deeply to learn what accounts for the passivity of many laymen and the bitterness of many others, for the identity crisis of some priests and the morale problems to which it seemingly gives rise, for the dearth of new priestly and religious vocations, and for the many continuing tensions and conflicts marring relationships between clerics and laymen.

Why do we not simply accept the fact that, in all the Church is and does, clergy and laymen play complementary roles? That priests and laymen, far from being locked in an endless struggle for power, absolutely require one another in order to live out their respective, God-given vocations? Why does the warning, decades after Vatican II, that we now face the twin perils of a "reclericalization of the Church" and the "secularization of the clergy" appear both apt and timely?[24] The answers lie in unlocking the riddle of clericalism.

First, though, we must recognize another grave problem arising from the same malignant source. The clericalist mentality shared by clerics and laity alike goes a long way to explain the failure of Catholic laymen to play the role that Vatican II envisaged for them in bringing Christian values to bear upon the institutions of secular culture. While perfect realization of the ideal proposed by the Council must no doubt forever elude our grasp in this present life, it is worth asking not merely why we fall short but why, today, American Catholics seem to be hastening in just the opposite direction. Here we touch upon the question of political engagement by the Church.

Over the last twenty years, acting through their national organizations, the National Conference of Catholic Bishops and the United States Catholic Conference, the bishops of

[24] Giovanni Magnani, S. J., "Does the So-Called Theology of the Laity Possess a Theological Status?" in René Latourelle, ed., *Vatican II Assessment and Perspectives: Twenty-Five Years After* (Mahwah, N.J.: Paulist Press, 1988), 590.

the United States, like their counterparts elsewhere, have spoken out forcefully and frequently on political, social, and economic matters. For the year 1988 alone, the table of contents of the standard collection of episcopal statements lists pronouncements on emergency hunger policy; civil rights; school-based clinics; homelessness and housing; military policy; federal funding of *in vitro* fertilization experiments; immigration policy; "food, agriculture, and rural concerns"; policy toward handicapped persons; sanctions for employers who hire undocumented aliens; developments in Eastern Europe and the Soviet Union; and comprehensive testimony to the Democratic and Republican party platform committees.[25]

Often, too, collective policy declarations of the bishops are followed up by detailed statements by individual bishops and members of the bishops' national staff as well as by implementing actions like congressional testimony and other forms of lobbying. As I write this, I have before me a United States Catholic Conference news release concerning a letter sent by an archbishop to the U.S. Senate and House agriculture committees about something called the "Pesticide Reform Act".

The issue here is not whether the archbishop's views on pesticides and the views of his episcopal colleagues on many other such matters are correct (no doubt they often are) or whether the bishops have a constitutional right to take these positions and publicize them (plainly they do). The difficulty is that, coming from the clerical hierarchy, this proliferation of sociopolitical judgments of a very specific nature is an expression of clericalism. Granted the right, and even the occasional obligation, of Church leaders to address such matters, *how* this routinely is done in the Church in the

---

[25] See Hugh A. Nolan, ed., *Pastoral Letters of the United States Catholic Bishops*, vol. 4, 1983–88 (Washington, D.C.: United States Catholic Conference, 1989).

United States exhibits the modern clericalist mentality at work.

Consider another archbishop's defense of the U.S. bishops' 1986 collective pastoral letter on economic justice, delivered to a delegation of politically and economically knowledgable, though conservative, laymen: "The Church has to insert itself into the national debate or else risk finding itself declared—properly—irrelevant."[26] Quite so. But is publishing a *bishops'* document on economic justice the only way to insert *the Church* into the policy debate? Suppose the bishops kept silent on the specifics of economic justice while the Catholic laity spoke out—would *the Church* then have no voice? No one doubts that bishops are part of the Church and play a leading role in her affairs; but it does not follow that, for the Church to speak and act, *they* always must speak and act. To suppose otherwise reflects the ecclesiology of clericalism.

As matters now stand, on sociopolitical issues the bishops judge and prescribe, and the Catholic laity, precisely as such, are silent. Indeed, on sociopolitical issues, the Catholic laity as such lack any corporate mechanism to formulate and express their views except insofar as these may be interpreted, mediated, and articulated by their clerical leaders. Meanwhile the real shapers of the secular political culture go on pursuing their own utilitarian aims in their own Machiavellian manner, with little regard for anything "the Church", however defined, has to say about issues and the bearing of moral principles upon them.

The problem is not confined to the Church in the United States. Consider the mind-set underlying this statement by an Argentinian proponent of liberation theology explaining why the Latin American clergy should not abandon the priesthood in order to take up the revolutionary struggle: "It is the Church that must proclaim and support this liberation, and the Church is in the eyes of the people permanently linked

---

[26] Archbishop Rembert Weakland, O. S. B., quoted in Paul Wilkes, "The Education of an Archbishop", *The New Yorker,* July 15, 1991.

to the image and function of the priest."[27] Of course, and the fact that even proponents of radical political activism equate Church and priest suggests how truly pervasive clericalism is.

To return to the case of the United States, however, someone might object that if the clerical hierarchy said less about politics and economics and social issues generally, it would lose such influence on the political process as it now has. Perhaps. It is more likely, though, that the bishops' present relative lack of influence reflects the widely held perception that, when push comes to shove, they do not represent the Catholic laity in the political arena—they cannot deliver the votes.[28] The unhealthy situation now prevailing will not be remedied as long as clericalism remains in place.

The immediate need is not for the clerical hierarchy simply to walk away from sociopolitical commitments but for it to make room for laymen to share, on an equal footing, in the process by which the Church's political agenda is hammered out, communicated, and implemented. This obviously will require far more than simply expanding the role already played by the clericalized lay cadres who generally staff the ecclesiastical bureaucracy at the diocesan and national levels.

Beyond that, bishops and priests should make it their specific task to *teach* the Church's social doctrine to the laity (and perhaps first to master it themselves, if they have not done so), communicating it in all its richness and complexity rather than, as is now commonly done, merely mining magisterial documents for proof texts in support of particular policies and pieces of legislation commended to them by their staff. Among other things, teaching social doctrine will *extend* the clergy's influence, not diminish it, while at the same time

---

[27] Quoted in Gustavo Gutierrez, *A Theology of Liberation* (Maryknoll, N.Y.: Orbis, 1973), 122, n. 18.

[28] See, e.g., Timothy A. Byrnes, *Catholic Bishops in American Politics* (Princeton, N.J.: Princeton University Press, 1991), 36–37.

it satisfies the laity's right to sound catechesis on the one hand and to autonomy in their areas of secular competence on the other.

In proposing solutions, however, I am getting ahead of my story. At this stage, the questions remain: What is clericalism, and what harm does it do? Consider this. Inappropriate clerical interventions in political and economic affairs usurp the role of the laity and discourage laymen from meeting their responsibility to shape secular culture in light of the gospel. Partly as a result, liberal secularism, not Christianity, is the dominant culture-forming force in the United States and other Western countries.

Even that may be putting it too optimistically. Western liberal secularism at least possesses a residue of moral principles inherited from Christianity. However, a correspondent of mine living in one of the cultural capitals of the nation contends that the emerging problem today is no longer secular humanism—"a dusty old faith held only by a handful of dusty old professors"—but something more ominous. "What I see around me", he writes, "is outright paganism."

On the level of personal morality, legalism operates as a kind of analogue of clericalist political activism in the realm of social morality. Legalistic clerics claim for themselves an authority they do not possess and use it to discourage and override the exercise of responsible decision making by the laity.[29]

Legalism is essentially the view that specific moral norms are more or less like positive laws or rules—that is to say, they are legislative enactments that can be revised, suspended, or even taken off the books by a qualified lawgiver. Religiously minded legalists typically consider God to be the ultimate lawgiver, and of course this is correct—God *is* the source of moral law—provided one understands what "law" and "law-

---

[29] See Germain Grisez, "Legalism, Moral Truth, and Pastoral Practice", *Anthropotes* 6, no. 1 (1990): 111–21.

giver" mean in this unique context: not law on the model of human positive law, subject to amendment or repeal, but moral *truth* embodying what is necessary for the integral fulfillment of man.

Legalists fail to grasp this crucial fact about morality and moral norms. Thus they also fail to recognize the intrinsic connection between leading a morally good life—a life of choices and actions consistent with moral truth—and human fulfillment. As a result, hell becomes an extrinsic punishment, imposed by God, and a good life a mere means to gaining a heavenly reward.

Legalism most dramatically makes common cause with clericalism in the attitude that the Church's moral doctrine is something like a body of positive law whose interpretation and application are entrusted to the members of a professional, clerical elite.[30] In the past, this view was expressed in various ways: obedience was valued above charity; the emphasis in moral teaching and guidance was upon the minimum required to avoid mortal sin; the quest for holiness was thought to concern only priests and religious; the positive content of the lives of laymen—work, marriage, and so on—was seen as having little religious significance.

It was a central principle of this way of thinking that doubtful laws do not bind (which is true enough where positive laws are concerned but beside the point where the issue is moral truth). Pastors and confessors imbued with legalism sometimes even imagined that they had the power to dispense (or refuse to dispense) from a variety of moral obligations.

This is not merely a description of the Catholic past. Legalism flourishes in the Church today. Dissenting theologians and pastors suppose themselves to be engaged in a crusade

---

[30] Since I do not care to waste time on easy targets, let me only observe in passing that this also is the attitude underlying liturgical abuses by priests: "The liturgy is *mine* inasmuch as I am a priest, and I can change it to suit my personal taste."

to liberate Catholics from legalism, but legalism pervades their own mentality.

Uniformly, they regard even correct and valid moral norms as rules formulated to protect underlying values; and since it is the *values,* not the *norms,* that ultimately are important, the norms—being only rules—always can be amended or set aside when that seems necessary for the sake of realizing some greater good or lesser evil. As for moral norms that they do not accept, dissenting theologians and pastors consider them outdated, or simply erroneous, rules that the Church should change and treat them as such in their teaching and pastoral practice.

Legalistic assumptions were strikingly reflected in the frequent speculation, before the publication of the encyclical *Humanae Vitae* in 1968, about whether Pope Paul VI would "change" the Church's teaching on contraception. They are reflected today in repeated references to the Church's "ban" on such practices as abortion and remarriage after divorce. (Bans, after all, are legislative enactments—rules—which can be changed.) They are part of the mind-set behind the phrase "the Church's *official* teaching" (on birth control, homosexual sex, or whatever it might be), which in contemporary Catholic discourse often means "the rules of behavior that the Pope and the bishops presently insist upon but that can and should be changed—and that, pending change, can safely be ignored". They underlie pastoral use of "internal forum" solutions in marriage cases that should be dealt with by determining the truth about the status of the persons involved. They account for the advice often given to laymen who find it hard to observe some element of the Church's moral doctrine to "follow conscience" (i.e., "take *my* advice") rather than the teaching of the Church.

This is not the place for a refutation of legalism, whether it be the legalism of the past or today's "pastoral" version. My point is only that legalism has done, and goes on doing, great harm to the lives of Catholics. And although legalistic thinking is not a product only of clericalism, still the clericalist mentality, with its distorted notions about the spiritual "power" of the clerical caste, found it congenial in the past and continues to do so today.

What about clericalism and sanctity?

In a 1935 encyclical on the priesthood, Pope Pius XI cited a section of the 1917 Code of Canon Law affirming that, both interiorly and exteriorly, the lives of clerics must be more holy than the lives of laymen.[31] This is a view commonly held not only in the past but also in the present.

Who would question the proposition that clerics should lead holy lives—that, indeed, they should be saints? But this also is true of laymen. Even when cast in terms of duty, the casual assumption of spiritual superiority on the part of clerics (and religious, considered as a kind of clerical auxiliary corps) is not just troubling in its practical implications but also hard to square with the teaching of Vatican II: "All the faithful of Christ of whatever rank or status are called to the fullness of the Christian life and to the perfection of charity. . . . In the various types and duties of life, one and the same holiness is cultivated by all."[32]

Whatever effect exhortations to spiritual superiority may have upon clerics, for laymen they easily translate into an invitation to spiritual mediocrity. This was true in the past, and it remains true today. It is still another product of clericalism. Most people would probably agree that priests *should* lead holier lives than the laity; the corollary, as far as the laity are concerned, is that the Council's universal call to holiness goes unheeded by many.

Of course, only God has certain knowledge of the state of souls. Ultimately, the rest of us are in the dark where sanctity and the interior lives of individuals—in many respects,

---

[31] *Ad Catholici Sacerdotii*, 26.   [32] *Lumen Gentium*, 40, 41.

even our own—are concerned. But plainly there is no reason for *optimism* about the present state of American Catholic spirituality as it is reflected in such things as the declines in Sunday Mass attendance and reception of the sacrament of penance since 1960, the falloff in priestly and religious vocations, and the documented rejection by many persons who identify themselves as Catholics of major elements of the dogmatic and moral content of their Faith.

Something Dietrich Bonhoeffer once said, speaking of the Christian Church generally, helps explain what has happened: "By thus limiting the application of the commandments of Jesus to a restricted group of specialists, the Church evolved the fatal conception of the double standard—a maximum and minimum standard of obedience."[33] Whether or not the blame for this situation should be laid precisely at the feet of the "the Church" (I would prefer to say "the clericalist mentality"), Bonhoeffer is here describing a painful reality. The "specialists" in his account are the clergy and their auxiliary corps, the nonordained religious, while those thought to be held to only a "minimum standard" are the laity.

This point is relevant to the current Catholic controversy over women's ordination to the priesthood. Clerical elitism is not the direct source of the women's ordination movement, which has its roots in feminism; but, in the Catholic context, clericalism adds a special dimension to the debate—in fact, two special dimensions.

The first concerns the fact that, as we shall see, the clericalist mentality distorts the idea of power in the Church by interpreting it in political terms—domination and submission—rather than in terms of service. Those who argue for women's ordination routinely speak of the need to empower women. Indeed, to the extent that clericalist attitudes persist, this cry for em-

[33] Dietrich Bonhoeffer, *The Cost of Discipleship*, in John De Grucy, *Dietrich Bonhoeffer: Witness to Jesus Christ* (London: Collins, 1988), 160.

powerment points to a real problem. In a clericalist setting, a woman (or man) who is not a priest can expect to be excluded from decision making unless she (or he) is willing to pay the price of admission by being clericalized—that is, by adopting clericalist attitudes and values.

But the clericalist mentality also is at work in the women's ordination controversy at a deeper level. At the heart of clerical elitism, as we also shall see below, lies the idea that the priestly vocation is the ideal for everyone: the life-style of the ordained priesthood, one might say, defines the Christian norm for every member of the Church. But if that is really so, then any Catholic woman who is serious about loving and serving God as well as she can *should* desire ordination—just as, for that matter, any Catholic man should do.

It is not helpful to tell such women that they do not have vocations to the priesthood. Of course they reject the idea, but it would not improve the situation if they agreed. For when it is interpreted from a clericalist perspective, this message—"You do not have a vocation"—simply shifts the blame from man to God. Would not God be the ultimate sexist in refusing to call women, merely on the basis of gender, to that way of life—the ordained priesthood—that represents the ideal for all?

If this analysis is correct, those who believe (as I do) that the Church, by the will of Christ, is unable to ordain women as priests must recognize that this controversy will not, and indeed cannot, be settled until the Church comes to grips with clericalism. It often is said that denying ordination to women contradicts neither their dignity nor their equality with men, and essentially that is true. But where the men in question are *clerics,* clericalism undercuts this argument by affirming, either subtly or openly, that at least *these* men are superior.

By now, one basic fact should be clear. Clericalism in all its forms and manifestations has done and goes on doing great harm to all the members of the Church individually, priests as well as laity, and also to the Church as a whole. It is systemic and pervasive. Until it is recognized and eradicated, it will continue to poison Catholic life in countless ways.

Where shall we look for solutions?

Much of this book is concerned with answering that question. But let me lay my cards on the table at the start and point out, in general terms, where the solution really does lie.

First of all, it is necessary to stop thinking of the clergy-laity distinction as if it expressed all that needs expressing about the fundamental structure of the Church. From a certain point of view, the Church *is* divided into clerics and laymen, and this *does* represent the will of Christ. Nothing that follows should be understood in a sense contrary to the explicit statement of Canon 207.1: "By divine institution, among Christ's faithful there are in the Church sacred ministers, who in law are also called clerics; the others are called lay people." But this division of the community of the faithful is not ultimate and exhaustive.

More basic than any state of division within the Church is a fundamental *undivided* state of the Christian community. This is not merely a theoretical construct but can actually be discerned in the condition of those newly initiated into membership in the community by baptism. In ecclesial terms, this is the condition of the Church herself understood as *communio*, a community of persons in communion with God whose mutual relationships are best understood on the model of the Trinity itself.[34]

This points to a simple but indispensable conclusion: it is imperative to give renewed emphasis, in true and appropriate ways, to the radical oneness and equality of all the members of the Church arising from baptism. In our thinking and our practice, we need to offset the bipolarity of the Church's

[34] See *Christifideles Laici*, 18.

division into clergy and laity with this vision of the radical unity and equality of all the *christifideles,* Christ's faithful people. In fact, considering that its neglect for many centuries does much to explain the debilitating state of mind called clericalism, we need now to give particular emphasis to the radical unity and equality of all.

The unity and equality of the *christifideles* have startling, dynamic implications. On this basis, it becomes possible for clerics and laymen to discern and live out their proper vocations and ministries in ways that are not only harmonious but also mutually complementary. From this perspective it is clear that the complementarity and interdependence of the Church's lay and clerical members are not merely sociologically convenient but also intrinsic to the very nature and being of the Faith community and the *christifideles* themselves. In speaking of such "community" values, we are speaking not just of the requirements for pleasant relationships within this or any other social setting but of what is absolutely necessary to realize the identity of cleric and layman.

The International Theological Commission makes this point in its document on priestly ministry: "Thus, the people cannot exercise their ministry without [a] priestly minister, but, similarly, the latter—bishop or priest—cannot fulfill his priestly office without the people, for he exists only in the priestly community. 'No Church without bishop and no bishop without Church', said St. Cyprian."[35] The thrust of clericalism, however, is precisely to place exaggerated emphasis upon the clerical hierarchy (and very little upon the lay faithful), while the contrary thrust of neocongregationalism, reacting against clericalism, is precisely toward a Church without a hierarchy.

Implicit in the ecclesiology of the Church as *communio* is an understanding of vocation that sees this term standing for

[35] In Sharkey, 52.

three related but distinct realities: (1) the baptismal or common Christian vocation, which marks the initiation of Christian life and is oriented absolutely and intrinsically toward "the acquiring of fullness of life in Christ";[36] (2) vocation in the sense of a divine summons to what are usually called states of life (priest, religious, married layman, etc.) but that a correspondent of mine cogently argues ought more properly be called various forms of "special service"; and (3) unique individual vocation. It is vocation in this third sense—unique individual vocation—that is especially relevant to solving the problem of clericalism.

For all members of the Church, their individual vocations define both their individual status and their individual duty. Typically, however, clericalism goes wrong by overemphasizing the role of vocation in the second sense (state of life), while congregationalism and neocongregationalism err by placing exaggerated emphasis upon vocation in the first sense (the common, baptismal vocation). Clericalists make too much of the clerical vocation, congregationalists of the vocation that is common to all. In both cases the remedy lies in grasping the importance of unique individual vocation. Only within the framework supplied by this personalist emphasis do "vocations" in the other two senses (baptismal calling, state in life) come into a functional synthesis in the lives of individuals.

It is a fundamental assumption of clerical elitism that the clerical state embodies an ideal that is in a sense normative for all members of the Church. Not that clericalists expect or want everyone to be priests—far from it. But they do suppose that the clerical life-style is the standard for measuring and judging all other Christian life-styles.

That accounts for a widely held view of the lay state: it is a compromise solution for Catholics who lack what it takes

[36] Vatican Council II, *Unitatis Redintegratio*, 22.

to become priests or religious.[37] Laymen then are judged, and the clericalists among them judge themselves, to be successes or failures, praiseworthy or blameworthy, according to how well they mirror the clerical ideal.

It is also suggested[38] that clericalism arises from a false idea of mediation: the priestly mediator *replaces* Jesus, assumes his powers, does his work; while the nonordained, the laity, are considered to be essentially passive. We shall see that the authentic idea of clerical mediation resides in the priest's acting *in persona christi* in a special and precise sense—a quasi-sacramental mediation, by which the priest acts as Jesus' proxy, not *replacing* him but making his action present here and now. "Present" for what? For the active participation and cooperation of the Christian community, the *christifideles* generally. This is a prescription not for imposing passivity on the laity but for establishing the conditions for their participation in the action and mission of Christ.

No one is really to blame for the persistence of the strange ideas reflected in clericalism and its offshoots. They are part of the religious culture that Catholics imbibe from infancy on and grow up taking for granted as part of the natural order of things. They are at least as widespread among laymen as among the clergy. They exist among both liberals and conservatives. In fact, one of the odder phenomena of the years since Vatican II has been the emergence of liberal Catho-

---

[37] Plainly, when it comes to situating religious life in its scheme of things, there is a certain lack of clarity in the clericalist mentality. In general, the religious life is subsumed as a kind of subspecies of the clerical life: women religious are viewed more or less as female auxiliaries to the priesthood, while nonordained male religious are mostly ignored. As against the laity, religious are identified with the clergy; as against priests, those who are not ordained are less than full members of the clerical caste. Of course this is an absurd view of religious life—but it is not my purpose to defend clericalism's acuity and grasp of the natures and implications of diverse vocations.

[38] By Germain Grisez, in correspondence with the author.

lics every bit as clerical-minded as Newman's critic George Talbot.

In the past as well as in the present, of course, many Catholics have reacted against clerical elitism, and not a few have become apathetic, cynical, and alienated from the Church. Such reactions are themselves products of clericalism that often coexist with persistent clericalist attitudes and assumptions among those who are alienated and disoriented. The "spoilt priest" is after all a stock figure among Catholic character types.

Sometimes clerical elitism is capable of expressing itself in ways that are actually rather amusing. Consider Henry Morton Robinson's 1950s bestseller, *The Cardinal*. The novel concerns a talented clerical careerist, Stephen Fermoyle, who climbs the rungs of the ecclesiastical ladder to very near the top. At story's end Fermoyle, by now a cardinal, is standing on the deck of a transatlantic liner, thinking of other clerics he has known and of their role in human affairs: "Across the desolate shingle of the world, priests would move among erring, afflicted men and women, comforting their sorrow, counseling them against despair, teaching them to support each other in acts of loving-kindness, pleading with them to accept some fragment of grace or receive—amidst scenes of mortal decay—some intimation of their immortality."

Although the prose is oppressively rococo, this vision of priestly ministry has much to recommend it. Less commendable, however, is what follows:

> "Father", men called them. O most trusting of names—an echo of the Name uttered by circling choirs of seraphim, by souls clinging to the cliffs of purgatory, by bereaved children of Adam weeping and wailing in this valley of tears. A Name repeated ceaselessly in monodies of praise by lynx and leviathan, by inchworm, wind, and wave. A Name trumpeted by the hurricane, flashed in the lightning's code—a Name boiling at the volcano's heart, and roaring above the avalanche.

> ... As the ship entered the narrowing defile of ice, Stephen lifted that Name in utter dependence and trust: "Our Father".[39]

Leaving aside the religiosity of lynxes and leviathans, when a popular writer sees nothing incongruous in so confusing the identities of the priest and the First Person of the Trinity, one can reasonably conclude that something, somewhere, may perhaps have gotten slightly out of whack.

No one in our less ingenuous age is likely to fall into such errors of rhetorical excess. Today's approved style requires bending over backward to avoid sycophancy toward clerics. A knowledgeable and up-to-date Catholic layman adopts a leveling tone: "Father Bill" (or just plain Bill) "is a guy just like the rest of us." And of course that is true enough. Yet beneath the surface of this superficial egalitarianism, clericalism and its radically impoverished idea of vocation continue to thrive. There are many signs of that.

Consider how we all are accustomed to use the word "vocation". The current shortage of new candidates for the priesthood is "*the* vocations crisis". Efforts to recruit candidates are "vocations programs". Church personnel responsible for this work are "vocations directors". The message is that a vocation is a calling to the clerical state.

Such attitudes flourish even—or should one say especially?—at the extreme fringes of neocongregationalism. For instance, "[M]ore and more parishes and dioceses are appealing today to lay persons to distribute communion. . . . This small intrusion cracks the entire edifice: a power ceases to be absolute as soon as, in any moment of its activity, some power (however limited) escapes from it. The monopoly is quite simply denied."[40] In other words, the real issue in the relationship between clerics and laity ultimately is "power" and who exercises it; even a seemingly minor innovation like letting laymen distribute communion gives them a leg

---

[39] *The Cardinal* (New York: Simon and Schuster, 1950), 511.
[40] Parent, 120–21.

up in this contest, for in such ways the power monopoly of clerics is undermined—understandably so, since advancement for the laity lies in looking and acting more like clergy and thus acquiring clerical power.

Is this, one might ask, really what contemporary Catholic life is all about? Are these really the issues that should engage our attention?

But they do.

To a great extent, the solution to the problems arising from clericalist attitudes lies in the fact that laymen have authentic vocations in all three senses: the common baptismal vocation, vocation as state in life or special service, and unique individual vocation. Much that follows will be concerned with that reality and its implications. But before considering how to escape from the dead end of clericalism, we need to see how we got here. Let us turn to a brief history of Catholic clericalism and how it grew.

II

A BRIEF HISTORY OF CLERICALISM

What follows can be called a "history" only with tongue in cheek. Tracking clericalism over the centuries is too vast a task for this modest volume. I mean only to highlight a few episodes and trends, leaving the serious work to historians.

In very general terms, then, the historical record suggests that the problem of clericalism has to do with the world. Not just the world as it is, though that certainly is part of it, but especially "the world" as Christians sometimes have tended to think of it.

A personal anecdote will illustrate what I mean.

Years ago I spoke at a Catholic seminary's conference on lay spirituality. It was a subject on which I soon showed myself singularly unqualified to have an opinion, for essentially I argued that there is no such thing as a spirituality for laymen. Priests and religious have the real interior lives. At most, the laity now and then may take themselves out of their normal secular environments—family, job, the world—in order to act like monks and nuns. Otherwise, lay spirituality had really to be considered beyond their reach.

There were, I pointed out, just too many obstacles, and the largest was precisely this entity called the world. It was large, noisy, confusing, full of distractions and temptations. As a factor in the lives of Christian laymen, it had but two functions: to be a place where you learned to say no—where doing good *was* avoiding evil; and to be shunned, fled from as much as possible, in order to lead a poor imitation of the monastic life in whatever odd corners of time and circumstance you might snatch for the purpose.

I was scarcely the only person to think that way. Indeed, I was simply parroting what for a long time had been one prevailing view of the world, the spiritual life, and the awkward situation of laymen in regard to both. I was saying what had been said often before: the world is dangerous to the spiritual health of Christians, and people seriously concerned with saving their souls do well to remove themselves from it as much as they can.

This attitude has many sources, though some, upon closer examination, do not really support it—for example, Romans 12:2: "Do not be conformed to this world." Saint Paul is making an important point. But what is it? Vatican II explains: "By the world is here meant that spirit of vanity and malice which transforms into an instrument of sin those human energies intended for the service of God and man."[1]

Exactly. And I had supposed that this sums up the world's total significance for Christian life. The Council views it differently: "Redeemed by Christ and made a new creature in the Holy Spirit, man is able to love the things themselves created by God, and ought to do so. . . . Grateful to his Benefactor for these creatures, using and enjoying them in detachment of spirit, man is led forward into a true possession of the world."[2]

Why, we may ask, have Christians not always grasped this? For the answer, we must go to our Christian roots.

In criticizing clericalism, it is important to avoid idealizing the situation of the laity in the early Church, as if this were the definitive golden age in the relationship between clerics

---

[1] *Gaudium et Spes*, 37.   [2] Ibid.

and laity. In fact, we do not know enough about it to reach any such conclusion. Still, the situation in those early years clearly was very different from what it came to be over the centuries and has largely remained up to now.

As the International Theological Commission points out, the New Testament in many places shows the apostles choosing collaborators and passing on to them a variety of ministerial functions. In these one discerns the threefold ministry of Christ as Prophet, Priest, and King: "The role of the ministers appointed by the apostles to be their collaborators is defined in the first place by the proclamation of the Gospel. . . . But it includes also the direction of liturgical service (1 Tim 3:9; 4:13) and the activity of guiding the community (1 Tim 3:15; 5:17–19; cf. 1 Pet and the pastoral letters)."[3]

Against leveling claims about the early Christian community put forward to support the neocongregationalist hypothesis, a recent historian of the priesthood writes: "The view that the New Testament indicates that the total community was enjoined to celebrate the Eucharist, so that in principle any baptized Christian might be the eucharistic celebrant, appears to be totally without any foundation. . . . The earliest Church community is not an amorphous, acephalous congregation. Ministerial leadership in general is the basis for eucharistic leadership in particular."[4]

At the same time, the clergy-laity distinction, while obviously present, was not emphasized in the early Christian community as it would have to be in later centuries. Even the terms *priest* and *layman* are missing from the New Testament as names for distinct categories of persons within the community. No doubt the absence of the term *priest* is due partly to a desire not to confuse Christ's priesthood with the pagan priesthood or even, as the International Theological

---

[3] "The Priestly Ministry", in Sharkey, 45.

[4] Kenan B. Osborne, O.F.M., *Priesthood: A History of the Ordained Ministry in the Roman Catholic Church* (Mahwah, N.J.: Paulist Press, 1988), 80.

Commission says, with the Jewish priesthood. The latter had the character of a profession or inherited social role rather than a divine calling; moreover, by Jesus' time, its function had come to be mainly if not exclusively the offering of sacrifice. The early Christians, by contrast, had a clear understanding of Christ as the unique sacrificial mediator between humanity and God—the one who "offered for all time a single sacrifice for sins".[5] In this perspective, the reluctance of the early Christians to give the name "priest" to those among them who presided at their eucharistic liturgies is not difficult to understand.

It seems reasonable to suppose that this circumstance expresses something else as well: within the early Christian community, the clergy-laity distinction was balanced by a sense of the unity and radical equality of all within a hierarchical structure requiring diversity and complementarity of roles and functions. This is expressed strikingly in the Pauline metaphor of the Church as the Body of Christ. "Now there are varieties of gifts, but the same Spirit; and there are varieties of service, but the same Lord; and there are varieties of working, but it is the same God who inspires them all in every one. . . . For just as the body is one and has many members, and all the members of the body, though many, are one body, so it is with Christ. . . . If all were a single organ, where would the body be? As it is, there are many parts, yet one body. . . . Now you are the body of Christ, and individually members of it."[6]

Here the themes of unity, diversity, and complementarity of the members are synthesized in an organic image grounding the community's essential characteristics in a unique relationship with Jesus: "In the first Christian communities all believers formed the lot chosen by God, all were called to be saints, all were elected and all were equal in dignity."[7]

---

[5] Heb 10:12.

[6] 1 Cor 12:4–6, 19–20, 27.

[7] Alexandre Faivre, *The Emergence of the Laity in the Early Church* (Mahwah, N.J.: Paulist Press, 1990), 39.

This seems to have been true not only for the inward-looking life of the Christian community and its members' relationships with one another but also for the view of apostolic responsibility shared, at least ideally, by all. The famous Epistle to Diognetus (c. 200) depicts a body of believers who, by the testimony of their lives, give witness to pagans concerning their faith.

> Yet while they dwell in both Greek and non-Greek cities, as each one's lot was cast, and conform to the customs of the country in dress, food, and mode of life in general, the whole tenor of their way of living stamps it as worthy of admiration and admittedly extraordinary. . . . In a word: what the soul is in the body, that the Christians are in the world. . . . The soul, when stinting itself in food and drink, fares the better for it; so, too, Christians, when penalized, show a daily increase in numbers on that account. Such is the important post to which God has assigned them, and they are not at liberty to desert it.[8]

This may very well depict an ideal that often was far from being realized in fact; but, if so, it is no less significant that it was recognized as an ideal. That bears reflection at a time when assimilation into a pervasively secularistic culture is perhaps the largest problem facing the Catholic community in the United States and when many Catholics apparently continue to suppose that "preaching the gospel" and "spreading the Faith"—evangelization, in other words—are the responsibility of only priests and religious.

What happened?

Gradually a process of clericalization set in. No doubt there were many reasons, but no doubt, too, the most important causes were those rooted in human nature and human weakness: in the tendency to specialization existing in every society, and particularly in the tendency to shirk responsibility afflict-

---

[8] In Colman J. Barry, O.S.B., ed., *Readings in Church History* (Westminster, Md.: Christian Classics, 1985), 39–40.

ing most members of most groups—together with the praiseworthy willingness of the few to fill the vacuums created through such shirking by the many. Indeed, this general sociological truth has particular relevance precisely to this period in the Church's history, when the new experience of toleration and the rapid expansion that resulted led to the baptizing of substantial numbers of persons not yet fully formed in the Faith. Indirectly and over a period of time, in combination with other factors touched on below, the resulting situation contributed to the idea that only priests were committed to the fullness of the gospel.

The beginning of the third century marked a new stage in the lay-clergy relationship. At that time the term *lay* came into general use, while the idea of clergy was clarified and the word itself became common.[9] But something else besides this reasonable and necessary process of clarification also was occurring: the understanding that laymen and clerics had of themselves and of one another was changing and with it the relationship between these two now well-defined classes of Christians. "The layman was quite certainly regarded as inferior to the clergy at that time. . . . From this period forward, the layman's function was to release the priest and levite from all his material concerns."[10]

These trends were accelerated and greatly encouraged under Constantine and his successors. Although the process of clericalization already had begun before Constantine, from the time the emperor, newly converted to Christianity (312 A.D.), turned his attention to protecting and promoting the Faith he had embraced, it flourished even more.

There is nothing surprising about Constantine's intervention in the affairs of the Church. The Roman world of his time took it for granted that religion supplied the basic orientation of society's mores and institutions and that the Emperor himself had a primary role in guiding the state along these lines. Christianity nevertheless brought with it a revolution

[9] Faivre, 43.   [10] Ibid., 69.

in the Roman constitution: from this time on, as *pontifex maximus,* the Emperor no longer was supreme authority in what had now to be distinguished as spiritual matters.

In this new situation it could hardly have been clear to everyone just how the Emperor was to fulfill his responsibilities for the empire's well-being, including its fundamental religious institution. Constantine seems to have thought of himself as being, in some sense, a part of the Church's hierarchical structure and, according to one early biographer, referred to himself as "the bishop of external affairs".[11] On the Church's side, the main effort from now on was directed toward trying to keep it clear that there were two distinct authorities, the spiritual and the temporal, something by no means easy in a world where practically all matters were "mixed".

The constant temptation of almost all the emperors, encouraged by the Arian bishops, who constantly sought imperial support, was caesaropapism—the notion that the Emperor, as the one with overall responsibility for society as a whole, should also be the ultimate authority in the religious sphere. Not even the fall of the empire was to bring about an end to the confusion and conflict, since for the most part the successor kingdoms that dominated Europe for the next seven hundred years operated on the basis of the same caesaropapist assumptions.

As for clergy and laity, up to Constantine's time there had been few if any visible differences between their respective ways of life: "Presbyteroi and even some episkopoi continued to live as ordinary working men, tending their farms and businesses. Only in case of need did the local episkopos subsidize the presbyter. In most respects, sociologically, the presbyter was not differentiated from the lay person."[12]

This changed dramatically under Constantine and his successors. Of course, the distinct character of the ministerial priesthood has a theological foundation, and undoubtedly it

[11] Quoted in Faivre, 144–45.   [12] Osborne, 146.

was judged necessary to clarify the distinctively sacred character of the ordained priesthood in a world that tended to see the activities of priests as social services by state functionaries. Nevertheless, the impact of these innovations, especially as the numbers of converts greatly increased, inevitably contributed to the development of clericalism.

Clerics, at least those most directly concerned with worship, were exempted from civil and military service, from accountability to civil courts, and from the payment of civil taxes. Life-style distinctions became increasingly marked. From the fifth century on, priests began to wear distinctive garb outside the liturgy. Tonsure, at first observed only by monks, came to be prescribed around the year 400 more or less generally for the clergy. Councils of the fifth and sixth centuries taught the irrevocability of holy orders, and clerics were forbidden to resume lay life. And though continence seems to have been required of all priests from apostolic times, restricting the priesthood to the unmarried was increasingly canonically mandated.

A recent writer sums up the cumulative impact on the clergy: "Living apart from the general run of people, wearing identifying clothing, remaining unmarried, acceptance into a group which had only lifelong commitment allowable to it, tonsured, exempt from civil and military service, untouched by civil taxation, and out of the reach of civil courts—all this led to . . . a separated caste."[13]

Parallel changes occurred in worship. Altars were situated at the rear walls of churches, and it was there that priests led the laity in offering the Eucharist. The tendency more and more was to turn the Mass into a clerical action rather than an action of the Christian people led by their priest.

> The sheer size of some of the new basilicas meant that the liturgy became more often something merely to watch. . . . Factors such as the Patristic emphasis on the Mass as a sacrifice,

[13] Ibid., 148.

the reaction against Arianism, and the severity of penances given in "private" confessions, all contributed towards a trend away from receiving holy Communion. . . . The general populace, swelled by the Germanic conversions, tended to see the Mass more as a traditional religious ritual than something calling for personal involvement.[14]

Powerfully reinforcing these trends was the emergence of the "private" Mass, originally a monastic innovation, which one writer calls "the greatest single change in the West".[15]

Theologizing about priesthood reflected the new realities. As the separation of clergy from laity became more pronounced and the ecclesial role of the latter diminished, separation from the world more and more became the ideal for priests. Whatever all this may have implied for the clergy, the results for the laity are clear enough. "The layman found his field of action reduced to worldly affairs, with the disappearance of the sense of the laity's active participation in the field proper to the Church, which had been so lively in the early centuries; the Church's mission came to be identified almost exclusively with the ministry of the clerics, and Christian perfection came to be considered as something proper to clerics and religious."[16]

The rise and spread of monasticism are an important part of this story. It would be absurd to suggest that monasticism has not been an enormously positive force in Christian life from its beginning up to the present day, yet distortions and exaggerations of the monastic spirit have played a part in shaping unhealthy attitudes toward the world and, in convoluted fashion, fostering the emergence and dominance of clericalism.

Monasticism, already clearly visible in the Church by the

[14] Dunn, 80.

[15] Ibid., 82.

[16] Alvaro del Portillo, *Faithful and Laity in the Church* (Shannon, Ireland: Ecclesia Press, 1972), 17.

fourth century, was an outgrowth of two earlier phenomena: the much-admired *continentes* and virgins, who committed themselves to permanent continency for the love of God, and the anchorites or hermits, male and female, who fled into the desert to meditate, pray, and practice austerities in solitude; there were, it is said, some five thousand of these in the Egyptian desert by the year 325 A.D.

Neither movement was clerical in its origins. Indeed, "because it was fundamentally asocial, hermitism was incompatible with the service to the community for which the clergy was destined". And besides, "The desert called for a deeply committed way of life which was often in great contrast to the mediocre level of life of the local clergy and . . . far removed from the successful search for privileges that many members of the clergy undertook in an empire that was beginning to offer this to them."[17]

Early monasticism similarly attracted both laymen and clerics, equally drawn to what they perceived as a more demanding, more devout way of life. (But not in every case: the prestige attaching to monasticism seems to have led some to become monks without undergoing real conversion or making a commitment to a truly different mode of living.)[18] Gradually, however, ordination became normative for the members of male monastic communities, a change that had unanticipated—and, in some important ways, deleterious—consequences. "Before [the change] took place, a man was made a minister of the altar not only because he was regarded as worthy of it, but also because it was useful to the community. The merits of the candidate were valued essentially in their relationship to the common good." It had been taken for granted that laymen also could be exemplary Christians. But with the change, new attitudes emerged, "developing until the point was reached where those who were neither members of the clergy nor monks—in other words, those

---

[17] Faivre, 190.   [18] Ibid., 194.

who were called lay or secular—were regarded as less worthy".[19]

Meanwhile, too, the flourishing of monasticism was having its impact on the secular clergy: the ideal of monastic spirituality became the norm for clerics generally, a development with profound and long-lasting results. "Through the centuries," a recent writer observes, "monasticism has wielded a profound influence on the way the clergy lived."[20]

This monastic influence upon the ideal of the priesthood as a whole led in its turn to yet another development. The distinction between clerics and monks came to be blurred to such an extent that eventually, Congar remarks, "the triple division into lay people, clerics, and monks became, by a process of assimilation of clerics to monks and of monks to clerics, a double division into men of religion and men of the world".[21] Not only for clerics but especially for the laity, the result was what might be expected: "It was inevitable that clergy and lay became more and more separated. Clerical life moves even further away from the borders of ordinary lay life."[22] It is only a short step to the conclusion that Congar notes, citing Gratian and other sources: "The lay condition is presented as a concession to human weakness. . . . From the Christian point of view life in the world is a compromise. A Christian who is completely consistent with the gospel principles that he professes ought normally to leave the world. . . . The laity, concerned in temporal affairs, have no part in the sphere of sacred things."[23]

In this story the case of Saint Augustine (354–430) is crucial, not only because of his importance in himself but also because of the enormous influence he exercised upon subsequent

[19] Ibid., 196.
[20] Dunn, 79.
[21] Congar, 9.
[22] Osborne, 188.
[23] Congar, 12–13.

Christian thought. But it is necessary to understand that a great deal said and written lately about Augustine misrepresents him, out of ignorance or else out of ideological bias, which finds him a convenient whipping boy for complaints about Church teaching. He was a far greater, and far more balanced, thinker than such criticism chooses to recognize. Yet even so he plays a role in the emergence of clericalism.

Let us start with the question of how Augustine viewed the world and human life therein. It does not have a simple answer. Consider the definition of the "happy life", which he supplies in the tenth book of his *Confessions*. Not surprisingly, it is to be identified with God: "There is a joy that is not granted to the wicked, but only to those who worship you for your own sake, and for whom you yourself are joy. This is the happy life, to rejoice over you, to you, and because of you: this it is, and there is no other. Those who think that there is another such life pursue another joy and it is not true joy."[24]

Plainly, this vision of the happy life for men is part and parcel of Augustine's program for the deepening and radicalization of the Christian commitment of his contemporaries. *The City of God*, for example, was written soon after the barbarian sack of Rome (410 A.D.), precisely to make it clear that Christ had not come to save the Roman Empire—that the mission of Christianity and the fate of Rome by no means were identical. Similarly, that the "happy life" lies in God is a necessary corrective to the idea—all too common then and now—that happiness for men resides in merely temporal satisfactions.

Still, it not clear that men *can* directly choose the Good that is God as such: not that we do not want to or would not do it if we could. We are made in such a way, however,

---

[24] *The Confessions of St. Augustine*, John K. Ryan, trans. (New York: Doubleday Image Books, 1960), 251.

that our choices necessarily concern *human* goods, among them of course our relationship with God. Even where God is in question, we draw near or draw away through the use or misuse of creatures. Augustine no doubt would have agreed. But a passage like the one quoted above can nevertheless be read—or misread—as encouragement to leap over creatures and go directly to God. It is this notion that is significant for our purposes.

Again, there is the role played by Neoplatonism in the evolution of Augustine's thought. Neoplatonism assumes a hierarchical ordering of creation that assigns more value—indeed, more reality—to spirit and less to matter. What is material and temporal is not evil; it is merely of less importance and, as an ascetical consequence, should be progressively set aside by someone striving for perfection.

By no means was Augustine a Neoplatonist. To cite *The City of God* again, a great deal of the book is taken up with his refutation of just such Neoplatonist thinking, especially as it pertains to the human body.

Repeatedly, for example, he insists, against thinkers who would denigrate the body and suggest that those who rise from the dead will have no need or use for bodies, that for men the glorified life of heaven will be *bodily* life in glorified bodies: "All the limbs and organs of the body, no longer subject to decay, the parts which we now see assigned to various essential functions, will then be freed from all such constraint, since full, secure, certain and eternal felicity will have displaced necessity; and all those parts will contribute to the praise of God."[25] A fair reading of Augustine does not find in him the antibody mentality that his ideological critics seek to attribute to him. Quite the contrary.

But—and this is the relevance of Augustine to our theme—none of this means his thought had no clericalist consequences.

---

[25] *City of God*, xxii, 30, Henry Bettenson, trans. (London: Penguin Classics, 1984), 1087.

Already in his time, as we have seen, clericalism had begun to grow significantly. And precisely the radical eschatological focus of Augustine's writings—his emphasis upon whole-hearted conversion to God and upon fulfillment transcending earthly, temporal life—did contribute to the conclusion, among those who wished to take their religious commitment seriously, that they should leave the world and dedicate themselves to God and the Church by adopting some sort of clerical life-style. This was not a necessary result of the "happy life" as Augustine understood it, but it did tend to be one practical result. In this sense, and not because of some antihumanist strain intrinsic to his thought, Augustine's thinking played a role in the spread and entrenchment of clericalism.

Augustine's influence was vast and enduring. So was the influence of a radical *contemptus mundi* that may not have been his position but that nevertheless tended more or less to be identified with him. Very much in this tradition centuries later is a work like *The Imitation of Christ*. This fifteenth-century volume, itself enormously influential, contains many passages like the following: "This is the most noble and the most excellent wisdom that can be in any creature: by despising the world to draw daily nearer and nearer to the kingdom of heaven. . . . Study, therefore, to withdraw the love of your soul from all things that are visible, and to turn it to things that are invisible."[26] This embodies a deep Christian wisdom, yet the wisdom is obscured by the crabbed version of *contemptus mundi* brooding over the passage.

By the early Middle Ages, clericalism was solidly entrenched. Sociological realities—for example, that clerics were virtually the only people to receive any formal education while most of the laity remained unlettered—go far to explain this. With the collapse of the Roman Empire and the rise of the barbarian

---

[26] Thomas à Kempis, *The Imitation of Christ*, Harold C. Gardiner, S. J., ed. (New York: Doubleday Image Books, 1955), 33.

successor states, the religious level of the new Christian converts, by comparison with the clergy who evangelized them, had declined precipitously, and with it expectations regarding what the laity could contribute to the life of the Church. The King became in effect the only layman with whom bishops and monasteries could treat as an approximate equal, and often even kings had hardly progressed in Christian terms beyond the minimal religious understanding required for baptism.

At the same time, sociopolitical circumstances also account for the fact that clericalism as we now think of it was by no means unchallenged. On the contrary, the era was marked by frequent, continuing tension and conflict between the clerical hierarchy and the lay lords, from Pope and Emperor on down. The roots of the struggle lay in the fusion of Church and state, which was universally taken for granted.

In the seventh and eighth centuries, for example, ecclesiastical property largely came under the control of the lay rulers, and parish priests were appointed by local lay authorities, a circumstance that naturally lowered their status in relation to the lords while tending to separate them from their bishops. The Church had entered the endless morass called lay investiture.

Yet it was also in the Middle Ages that the papacy most aggressively asserted its claims to temporal supremacy, claims that were based, in part at least, on the forged Donation of Constantine (c. 750–850), in which the great Emperor was supposed to have given ultimate authority over the empire to Pope Sylvester and his successors. The Donation is a fascinating document. For instance:

> We decree that those very reverend men, the clerics who serve the most holy Roman Church in various orders, shall have the same dignity, distinction, power and pre-eminence, by the glory of which our Senate is decorated; and we decree that the clergy of the most holy Roman Church shall be adorned as are the soldiers of the Empire; and just as the

> Imperial power receives dignity from various offices, chamberlains, doorkeepers and all the guards, so also we wish the holy Roman Church to be adorned; and so that the Pontifical dignity may shine forth more clearly, we decree this also, that the clerics of the same holy Roman Church shall decorate their horses with saddle-cloths of linen of the very whitest color, and thus the horses are to be equipped for riding; and just as our Senate uses sandals with fur covering, so let the clerics be distinguished by their very white linen; then shall terrestrial as well as celestial things be adorned to God's glory.[27]

In practical terms, however, the problem was not clerical domination of the laity but lay domination of the Church. The unique sacral role of universal responsibility accorded to the Emperor worked reasonably well when emperors were decent, God-fearing individuals like Charlemagne and his son Louis the Pious; but when they were not, the Church was subjected to the worst sort of vassalage. Indeed, lay investiture not only meant that the appointment of bishops and abbots had become a political matter but also that those appointed in many cases were hardly churchmen at all. For the Church as well as Europe as a whole, the later ninth and tenth centuries were true dark ages.

In this complex context, the reform movement within the Church associated with Pope Saint Gregory VII (1073–85) and the abbey of Cluny plays an important role in the evolution of clericalism. Reform was desperately needed, and among the highly desirable aims of the Cluniac and Gregorian program was to rescue the Church from the domination of lay lords and place her clearly under the authority of the Pope and the clerical hierarchy. Pope Gregory's sustained assault on lay investiture and his long conflict with the Emperor Henry IV were inevitable consequences of these efforts, which constitute a bright page in the history of the papacy.

But Gregory's principal weapon in his struggle to free the Church from lay control was the uncompromising assertion

---

[27] In Barry, 236–37.

of clerical supremacy over lay authority not only in ecclesiastical but also in temporal affairs. For the papacy he claimed supreme legislative and judicial authority; thus, when he excommunicated Henry IV (in the year 1080), he declared his adversary to be not only outside the body of the Church but also deposed as King of Germany and Italy. And indeed this made perfect sense in the context of church-state fusion: for Gregory's chosen means was to exercise his supreme spiritual authority by declaring that the subordinates of an emperor or king guilty of opposing the Pope in his pursuit of religious reform no longer were bound by the oath of vassalage—regarded by all as a religious act—which previously had bound them to their temporal ruler.

It may be, however, that the highwater mark for the assertion of clerical preeminence over the temporal order in opposition to lay domination of the Church was reached not in the eleventh century but in the thirteenth, with the publication of Pope Boniface VIII's bull *Unam Sanctam,* a tactical maneuver in the Pontiff's ultimately deadly conflict with the unscrupulous French King, Philip the Fair. Its famous passage on the "two swords" carries to dizzying heights the clerical claim to supremacy over the temporal order:

> And he who denies that the temporal sword is in the power of Peter, has wrongly understood the word of the Lord when He says: "Put up again thy sword into its place." Wherefore both are in the power of the Church, namely, the spiritual and material swords; the one, indeed, to be wielded for the Church, the other by the Church; the former by the priest, the latter by the hand of kings and knights, but at the will and sufferance of the priest. For it is necessary that one sword should be under another and that the temporal authority should be subjected to the spiritual.[28]

Pope Boniface lost his life for his pains, and even that, it can be argued, was part of the dynamic of clericalism. It is

[28] Ibid., 456.

no wonder that Church-state relations in the Middle Ages appear, at this distance in time, a gigantic muddle.

Yet even so, certain matters relevant to our subject are clear. One is that extreme assertions of clerical authority like Boniface VIII's "two swords" arose from a continuing struggle by the Church to oppose and break free from encroachments on her liberty and rights by lay powers. But even in this commendable effort the assumptions of clericalism can be seen at work. For although the struggle was fully justified, it is clear that in this context "the Church" signified the clerical hierarchy and *not* her lay members. That helps account for another, paradoxical fact. Clerical leadership led the way throughout these centuries in the long, painful, and entirely necessary effort to separate out the spiritual from the temporal. But one result of this process of separating out was to make "the Church" the preserve of clerics while divorcing "the temporal" from religious and spiritual influence. By the late Middle Ages, clericalism had helped set the stage for the division between the two, which has progressively deepened ever since.

In contrast, the thrust of medieval theological thinking about priests and priesthood was clear. According to the scholastic view, priests were ordained to celebrate the Eucharist, and the priest's identity came from his association with the sacrament. Saint Thomas Aquinas held that a priest essentially had two functions: celebrating the Eucharist and preparing the people to receive it.

This understanding of the priesthood can be caricatured and condemned as narrow, restrictive, and painfully limited, a view that reduces the priest to a sacramental functionary and makes of the priesthood a mere hieratic caste. But the critique's own theological understanding is much too shallow. Given the comprehensive character of the Eucharist as the sacrament that takes in the whole of Christian life so as to offer it to God united with Christ's priestly sacrifice, and given also the open-ended, outward-looking implications of "preparing" people to participate in the Eucharist, it is clear that a eucharistic theology of the priesthood opens the way to a ministry of great scope and intensity within the Christian community.

This is apparent from what Saint Thomas himself says on the subject: "But since the power of Order is directed to the dispensing of the sacraments, and since of all the sacraments the Eucharist is the most sublime and perfect, it follows that we must consider the power of Order chiefly in its relation to that sacrament. . . . Since then the power of Order extends to the effecting of the sacrament of Christ's body and the distribution thereof to the faithful, it follows that the same power should extend to the preparation of the faithful, that they be made fit and worthy to receive this sacrament."[29] Considering the matter from a sacramental perspective, Thomas situates the work of preparing the faithful to receive the Eucharist in the sacraments of baptism and penance; clearly, though, the work of preparation extends even further and offers priests the challenge of a rich ministry outside a formally sacramental framework as well as within it.

All the same, if this theological understanding of the priesthood focused upon the Eucharist is oversimplified (and in that way misrepresented), the results really can be unhealthy for both priests and laity. The situation existing by the time of the late Middle Ages is summarized by one writer this way:

> The Mass was now believed to produce spiritual benefits whether or not it was devoutly attended. "Private" Masses abounded. . . . By the fifteenth century, thousands of "altar priests" were being ordained just to say Masses—for the souls in purgatory, and for all manner of special intentions. . . . By the end of the Middle Ages, the Mass had been transformed from an act of public worship into a form of clerical prayer.

[29] *Summa Contra Gentiles*, iv, cap. 74, translation by the Dominicans, amended by C. Cronin in "The Sacrament of Order", George D. Smith, ed., *The Teaching of the Catholic Church* (New York: Macmillan, 1952), 1028–29.

> It had become a "good work", performed by priests for the spiritual benefit of the Church. This was the Mass the Reformers knew, and which many of them rejected.[30]

While the same writer maintains that this state of affairs was not so much the result of clerical domination as it was a consequence of "the people demanding these services of the clergy",[31] still, as Congar points out, parallel canonical developments did reinforce the passivity of the laity considered to be persons whose essential role was simply to receive the clergy's services. According to this canonical view, the laity are "negative creatures".[32]

The consequences for clergy and laity alike were distressing. As to the former, "Little by little, the awareness of the bond between the presbyterate and the 'service' of the people of God was lost; most priests no longer had any duty but to celebrate Masses, without the obligation to preach or instruct the people. As the benefice was no longer strictly connected with the pastoral duty, bishops themselves lost the sense of the duty to 'reside' among their flock."[33]

And the laity?

> In the Middle Ages the layman found his field of action reduced to worldy affairs, with the disappearance of the sense of the laity's active participation in the field proper to the Church, which had been so lively in the early centuries; the Church's mission came to be identified almost exclusively with the ministry of the clerics, and Christian perfection came to be considered as something proper to clerics and religious. The layman's possibilities were reduced to the practice of the common virtues in the exercise of his secular functions, which was generally presented in ascetic literature as an obstacle to the Christian life of perfection.[34]

---

[30] Dunn, 85.
[31] Ibid.
[32] Congar, 17.
[33] International Theological Commission, in Sharkey, 60.
[34] Del Portillo, 17.

This was part of the situation that Martin Luther and the other early Protestant reformers confronted. In the vehemence of their reaction against it, extending even to rejection of the priesthood and the Mass itself, one finds an explanation for the vehemence of the counterreaction embodied in the Council of Trent.

The congregationalism of the reformers, like today's neocongregationalism, clashes with definitive Catholic teaching as articulated both by Trent and Vatican II: that orders is a sacrament and that there is an essential difference between the ordained priesthood and the common priesthood. In seeking to collapse the distinction between baptismal priesthood and ordained priesthood, the contrary view unwittingly undermines the baptismal priesthood, whose claims it supposes itself to be advancing. The implication is that, in order to enjoy *real* ecclesial dignity, the nonordained must be priests just as much, and in *just the same way,* as the ordained are.

Trent's achievements in responding to the challenge were impressive. The Council (1545–63) definitively taught that orders is a sacrament; it unequivocally affirmed the uniqueness of ordained ministry and the spiritual powers of the priesthood; in many ways, it introduced clarity and urgently needed reform into the priesthood. On the practical level, this was especially true of the impetus that it gave to the seminary system for training the clergy. All this was to the good.

At the same time, one must acknowledge, as the International Theological Commission does,[35] that Trent, determined as it was to reaffirm and strengthen what the reformers challenged, did not go to the heart of the theological problems they had raised regarding priesthood and ministry. Today these same problems are reemerging in neocongregationalism and in other ways.

Moreover, in emphasizing the clergy while saying nothing

---

[35] See Sharkey, 13–15.

about the laity (because, presumably, nothing in the reformers' challenge specifically required that anything be said), Trent ushered in a long period during which the Church became further clericalized in theory and in practice. In sum, "the institutional, hierarchical aspect of the Church received all the attention, and the ordinary faithful were left in the shadows. With all this concentration on ecclesiastical authority and the hierarchy, it was inevitable that the Church would be seen as the domain of the clergy."[36]

There are some bright spots in this picture. For example, Saint Francis de Sales (1567–1622) directs his *Introduction to the Devout Life* to lay people and argues persuasively that the practice of heroic virtue is possible for the laity living in the world. Salesian spirituality, it is said, "while retaining much of the interior spirit of the desert, in the sense that a radical call from God does indeed claim and refashion the human heart, did not at all assert that that voice could only echo clearly in the stillness of the hermit's cave or the monastery cloister. That voice might also be raised and heard in a life lived in the midst of the world. . . . All walks of life provided suitable means for fashioning an authentic Christian way of being."[37] Similarly, Saint Ignatius Loyola's Spiritual Exercises were sometimes given to the laity and contain points for them.

But these were exceptions. "It is true that this aspect of holiness was never wholly absent," Congar remarks, "but Christians as a whole looked to a monastic spirituality and shared after a fashion in the monastic state."[38] Even the way of life of sincere Christian laymen in the world was viewed as "a sort of degenerate monastic life, which simply permitted

---

[36] Jordan Aumann, O.P., *On the Front Lines: The Lay Person in the Church after Vatican II* (Staten Island, N.Y.: Alba House, 1990), 8.

[37] Wendy M. Wright and Joseph F. Power, O.S.F.S., Introduction, *Francis de Sales, Jane de Chantal: Letters of Spiritual Direction* (Mahwah, N.J.: Paulist Press, 1988), 44–45.

[38] Congar, 410.

the married state and of which the part not given up to prayer, instead of being lived in the cloister under strict discipline of superiors, was lived at work and at home, but not out of sight of spiritual authority".[39] This view assumes that laymen are passive, subordinate objects of clerical ministration and authority within a clericalized Church.

Even so, common sense at this point requires recognition of an obvious, but easily overlooked, fact. Our sources for information about the religious situation of the Catholic laity in these centuries are found in theological, canonical, and ascetical literature. The view of laymen that emerges there is mainly negative. But no historical sources, and certainly not these, capture the totality of lived experience. Real life very likely differed significantly from the picture that emerges when one concentrates on situating the laity against the background of the pervasive clericalism in the Church.

Despite all that rightly can be said about the clericalist mentality of the times as reflected in writings of a theological, ascetical, and canonical nature, we can suppose that many laymen went unpretentiously about the business of living exemplary Christian lives in the service of their God, their Church, and their fellowman; that they were devout in their religious practices and conscientious in performing their secular duties; and that, however little esteem for the lay state theologians and theorists expressed, these lay people succeeded in discerning, accepting, and carrying out God's will as it was embodied in their personal vocations—of which a calling to the "lay state" was part—and, by doing so, grew into sainthood.

Still, the Church *was* clericalized. The institutional model described by Avery Dulles was dominant:

> The primary analogue for the theory of the Church as institution is . . . the secular State. The cleric accordingly comes to be viewed as a member of the ruling elite—a public officer

---

[39] Ibid., 411.

committed to the service of the institution and empowered to represent it officially. Under the impact of Greek hierarchical thinking, the clergy became a class that possessed total authority in the Church, so that no multitude or combination of the laity could exert even a modicum of power against the clergy. The clergy, by the perspectives of this theology, were thought to rule by divine right, just as in the secular State the kings and nobility were deemed to have their authority from God.[40]

This ecclesiological mind-set seems clear, for example, in the schema on the Church prepared for, but not acted upon by, Vatican Council I (1869–70):

> Christ's Church is not a society of equals as if all the faithful in it had the same rights; but it is a society in which not all are equal. And this is so not only because some of the faithful are clerics and some laymen, but especially because in the Church there is a power of divine institution, by which some are authorized to sanctify, teach, and govern, and others do not have this authority.... [T]he pastors and teachers appointed by Christ ... rule the Church of God with laws that are necessary and binding in conscience, with judicial decrees, and, finally, with salutary punishments for offenders even though they are unwilling; and this applies not only in matters of faith and morals, of worship, and of sanctification, but also in those matters which pertain to the external discipline and administration of the Church.[41]

There is a legitimate and important sense in which all of this is true. The Church is *not* a community of equals—not, at least, as "equal" is understood in simplistic egalitarian terms; all its members do *not* have the same rights; its pastors *do* have the authority and the duty to guide and direct it, even

---

[40] *Models of the Church* (New York: Doubleday Image Books, 1978), 168–69.

[41] In John F. Clarkson, S. J., John H. Edwards, S. J., William J. Kelly, S. J., and John J. Welch, S. J., *The Church Teaches: Documents of the Church in English Translation* (Rockford, Ill.: Tan Books, 1973), 93–94.

by correcting the erring. Hierarchical structure and the diversity of offices, charisms, and vocations within the community make it not only proper but also indispensable that there be differences among the members. But in the absence of affirmations concerning the necessary complementarity of diverse functions and concerning the radical unity and *equality* of all the faithful from the Pope to the humblest member of his flock—an equality based upon baptismal incorporation into Christ—affirmations of inequality, however true in principle, risk reinforcing both clerical elitism and lay passivity or alienation.

Somewhere in these centuries, too, another phenomenon began to appear, one that has proved to be among the most momentous of the modern era. At this point, we need to consider the relationship between the clericalist mentality and secularization, from the Renaissance through the Enlightenment to the French Revolution and on up to the present day.

As a result of the secularization process, positive interaction between secular culture and religion has diminished markedly in the West, with profound consequences both for society and for the lives of individuals. By no means has clericalism been the only cause of the secularization of Western culture, but clericalism, especially the clericalist/monastic version of *contemptus mundi* and the habits of thought and behavior it inspires, has played a role. The world, having for so long been treated with "contempt", made the interesting discovery that it was not only possible but also congenial for it to go its own way, at religion's expense.

The results have been alarming for both the Church and the world. Pope John Paul II, paying tribute in 1991 to Pope Leo XIII for the breakthrough in Catholic social doctrine accomplished a century earlier by the encyclical *Rerum Novarum*, notes that as recently as Leo's time a "twofold approach" to thinking about this world and the next was common in the Church: "One directed to this world and this life, to which faith ought to remain extraneous; the other directed toward a purely otherworldly salvation, which neither enlightens nor directs existence on earth".[42]

That had long been the case. For centuries, as Jacques Maritain pointed out, "Christian homiletic teaching was busy convincing men . . . that created things are worthless. . . . Simply through a phenomenon of inattention, a masked Manicheism was thus superimposed on the Christian Faith."[43]

And so, on the eve of our own era, a deep-rooted shakiness lay just below the apparently firm and monolithic surface of the ecclesiastical structure:

> The hostility of a civilization in which Christianity—and especially such a disfigured Christianity—was called to question on all sides, and where science was held to be the enemy of religion; the weakening of natural defenses due to modern psychasthenia . . . and the weakening of intellectual defenses due to a teaching extremely poor in matters of doctrine; the modernist crisis, with its first epidemic of itching ears and piously intended errors; and in the indispensable struggle against those errors, the almost exclusive recourse to disciplinary measures; the spiritual impoverishment of a Christian laity, who continued in general to imagine that the call to the perfection of charity, with what it implies of life of prayer and, as much as possible, of contemplative recollection, was the concern of the monks; the confusion and coalescence, which had been accepted as natural for two centuries, between the interests of religion and those of a social class furiously attached to its privileges.[44]

It is hardly surprising that reactions against this state of affairs now and then occurred. We have already seen something of clericalism's role in creating the ecclesial situation on the eve

---

[42] *Centesimus Annus*, 5.
[43] *The Peasant of the Garonne* (New York: Macmillan Paperbacks, 1969), 59.
[44] Ibid., 63.

A BRIEF HISTORY OF CLERICALISM

of the Reformation. But clericalism, especially of a politically oriented nature, made a comparable contribution to the rise of the virulently anticlerical European laicism that plays such an important part in continental cultural and political history well into the twentieth century. As Hilaire Belloc remarked of this phenomenon: "Anti-Clericalism may be defined as the spirit which is goaded into activity by the invasion of the civil province by clerical agency";[45] this spirit may be friendly enough to religion in its beginnings, but almost always it ends in deep hostility, not just to clericalism but also to all things religious.

Even among the more or less loyal laity and clergy of these times one finds evidence of what Maritain calls "an enormous weight of frustration, disillusionment, repressed doubts, resentment, bitterness, healthy desires sacrificed, with all the anxieties and pent-up aspirations of the unhappy conscience".[46] Let us take testimony on this matter from two nineteenth-century witnesses, Richard Simpson and Orestes Brownson.

With Lord Acton, Richard Simpson was coeditor of the *Rambler* when it fell afoul of the British bishops over a school question. Forced out of office in the maneuvering that briefly brought Newman to the editor's chair, he eventually poured out his anger in a long letter intended for publication, but not published, in a French journal. Simpson was a feisty individual, with a knack for giving and taking offense,[47] and his remarks resonate with the bitterness of a loser in the game of ecclesiastical politics—a contest often conducted with a genteel brutality surprising to outsiders. Still, one discerns here a sense of outrage that even more docile souls than Simpson's are likely to have felt at times.[48]

Describing the events at the *Rambler* as a "coup against

---

[45] *Survivals and New Arrivals* (New York: Macmillan, 1929), 122.
[46] Maritain, 63.
[47] Ker, 500.
[48] For substantial excerpts from this letter, see Coulson, 17–18.

the laity", he writes that "the English Hierarchy has been victorious; not over its enemies but over its friends. . . . They have triumphed over their own army, and have excited not the enthusiasm of Christian conquest, but the passions of civil war." He quotes a letter from another layman:

> This whole story is a warning to all who by writing or public life of any kind wish to serve the cause of religion as independent laymen, or in any other quality or office other than that of Bishops. If no other office is recognised, let us have it so declared. If all Catholic literature is to be confined to Bishops' Pastorals, and politics to be merely their echo, let it be known to all whom it may concern. If the dictum attributed to the Cardinal [Nicholas Wiseman], "the only function of the laity is to pay", be really the law of this land, let us know it, that we may get out of it into some more Christian country.

Simpson adds on his own behalf:

> This jealousy of the laity is a natural result of the strictness of the administrative organization which is now considered to constitute the strength of the clergy. . . . The compactness of the clerical union makes it a caste; it has a separate professional education and separate habits of thought. . . . The laity are to be kept in ignorance of all religious questions except those in the catechism, in order to misuse their obedience to a body of directors professionally educated to manage their religion for them. Religion is turned into administration, the clergy into theological police, and the body of thinking laymen into a mass of *suspects,* supposed to be brooding on nothing but revolution, and only kept together by motives of fear, and by the external pressure of clerical organisation.

This is very harsh. On the other side of the Atlantic, nevertheless, the convert apologist and social critic Orestes Brownson was reaching similar conclusions.

In an essay reflecting the American experience of church-state relations, which he published in July 1862,[49] Brownson

---

[49] "Lacordaire and Catholic Progress", in Alvan S. Ryan, ed., *The Brownson Reader* (New York: P. J. Kenedy & Sons, 1955), 341–48.

calls attention to the "great change" then occurring in "the mutual relations of the church and society" and declares the laity to be "much better prepared for it, and much more favorable to it, than the clergy".

Brownson was of course writing against the background of conflict between Pius IX and the laicist, anticlerical Italian nationalist movement. That conflict would end with the seizure of the Papal States and Rome, and with the Pope as the "Prisoner of the Vatican". Whatever Brownson may have thought about the events unfolding in Italy, however, he felt strongly that they should not exercise a controlling influence upon Catholic life in the United States; indeed, if the truth were told, this American experience had much to teach European Catholic defenders of the status quo.

Nevertheless, trying to strike an irenic tone, Brownson declares it "not fitting that the laity should array themselves against the clergy". On the contrary, "the great evil, and that which delays the change, is the attempts of the laity to accomplish [the new relationship between church and society] without this co-operation [of the hierarchy], and in spite of it. These attempts are impolitic, and even uncatholic."

Having made this concession, though, he lets his exasperation show. Contending that "the complete separation of church and state" is the best arrangement for both and that laymen have a right to hold and argue this point of view, he breaks out in terms not unlike Simpson's.

> I am bound to obey the pontificate, and to venerate the sacerdocy, both of which are from God, but I am not bound to take no thought for the interests of religion and society, or, in this country at least, to refrain from expressing my honest convictions, when they in no sense impugn Catholic dogma, or what is unchangeable in the constitution of the Church. There is a mission of genius, of intelligence in the church, which is not necessarily restricted to the clergy, and may be committed to laymen, or to clergymen in a sense outside of their sacerdotal character, for the church has the right to the service of the genius, the intelligence, the learning, the

good-will, and the zeal of all her members, of laymen as well as of clergymen.[50]

In the discussion of matters not yet settled by the authority of the Church, Brownson argues, "the layman, under responsibility . . . may take the initiative, and not await it from authority. He may open such questions as he deems important, and the business of authority is not to close his mouth, but to set him right, when and where he goes wrong." Then he says, with a typically American flourish: "What a crowned or a titled layman may do, a free American citizen, though uncrowned and untitled, may also do. I have as much right to make my suggestions, and offer my advice to the bishops or to the supreme pontiff as had Charlemagne and St. Louis, or as has Louis Napoleon or Francis Joseph to offer theirs. Before the church, if not before the state, all laymen are equal."[51]

All this Orestes Brownson claims for the Catholic laity as theirs by right. As a matter of fact, the existence of substantial lay rights already had been formally recognized—not only in practice but also in principle—at least once in the context of American Catholicism.

This happened in the 1820s in the diocese of Charleston, South Carolina, where, under the leadership of Bishop John England (1786–1842), a constitution for the governance of the diocese was adopted that even by today's standards seems advanced. By 1824 England was able to report to the Congregation for the Propagation of the Faith that this document "is now the standard for Catholics, and all our affairs in consequence thereof are progressing peacefully".[52]

England had been sent to Charleston as bishop in part at

[50] Ibid.
[51] Ibid.
[52] Quoted in Peter Clarke, "John England: Missionary to America, Then and Now", in Gerald P. Fogarty, S. J., ed., *Patterns of Episcopal Leadership* (New York: Macmillan, 1989), 78.

least to settle the controversy over lay trusteeism. Still, it seems that his diocesan constitution was more than just a tactical compromise intended to placate dissenters and those in sympathy with them. Describing the constitution as embodying "the heart of [England's] style of episcopal leadership", a recent writer says it takes for granted both "the need for a visible [local] Church" and the need for visible collaboration among her members. "This church would have a visible unity within itself and with the Catholic churches around the world. It would seek to be self-sufficient in regard to resources and ministers and to develop an indigenous clergy. Both ministry and decision-making would be guided by a spirit of cooperation, communication, consultation, and subsidiarity. . . . It is through the Constitution that [England] gave the members and the local congregations voice and vote in the direction of the building of the church."[53]

While Bishop England's constitution is a fairly comprehensive document, whose first two (of seven) articles enumerate the fundamentals of Catholic doctrine, for our purposes its treatment of laymen is of particular interest. The article on property not only speaks of the need to support the Church but also vests ownership of property in the diocese's general trustees: the bishop as president; the vicar as vice president; three clergymen chosen by their fellow clergy at an annual diocesan convention; six laymen also selected at an annual convention by a house of lay delegates; and a treasurer appointed by both houses—clergy and lay delegates—voting together.

Under this constitution, the power to establish "district churches" or local congregations and to name their pastors rests with the bishop; each, however, is to have a vestry, with the pastor as president but with the other members elected by the laity and comprising "discreet, well-conducted men having a regard for religion, and if possible, persons

[53] Ibid., 71.

who are in the habit of receiving the sacrament of the Holy Eucharist". The vestrymen have the duty to "exert themselves to procure for the Bishop and the clergymen of their own district decent and comfortable support; to have the Church and other buildings to be kept in good order and repair . . . to provide and keep in good order a burial ground for the interment of members in the communion of the church . . . and to see that the church property entrusted to their care be well preserved and improved and faithfully administered". The vestrymen are to choose the parish organist, clerk, sexton, and other staff and officials.

Members of the local congregations also elected delegates to the annual diocesan convention, described by the constitution in these terms:

> The Convention is not to be considered as a portion of the ecclesiastical government of the Church; but the two houses [clergy and laity] are to be considered rather as a body of sage, prudent and religious counsellors to aid the proper ecclesiastical governor of the church in the discharge of his duty, by their advice and exertions in obtaining and applying the necessary pecuniary means to those purposes which will be most beneficial, and in superintending the several persons who have charge thereof; to see that the money be honestly and beneficially expended.

The convention was competent to involve itself in more than temporalities, however. In fact, "In those cases where the Convention has no authority to act, should either house feel itself called upon by any peculiar circumstances to submit advice, or to present a request to the Bishop, he will bestow upon the same the best consideration at the earliest opportunity."

Although England's constitution had the approval of the Holy See and was viewed by the bishops at the First Provincial Council of Baltimore (1829) as at least an acceptable governance model for the diocese of Charleston, it did not serve as a model for other dioceses. That model instead was shaped largely by the determined efforts mounted by Church authorities throughout much of the nineteenth century to suppress lay trusteeism and, once it had been suppressed, to make certain that nothing like it ever again would rear its head in U.S. Catholicism.

Trusteeism seems to have made its first appearance in this country in the late eighteenth century, a creature of Irish Catholic immigrants who brought with them an experience of *de facto* church-state separation along with a marked lack of sympathy for what they perceived as a monarchical episcopacy. Typically, upon arrival they bought land, built churches, incorporated the property—"and then demanded the right to appoint pastors. Lay trusteeism had begun."[54]

Trusteeism emerged in New York and Philadelphia, where it became a vexatious problem for the new nation's first bishop, John Carroll. Indeed, it had been among the reasons leading the clergy in Maryland and Pennsylvania to petition Rome for the appointment of a bishop. For his part, Carroll recognized certain rights of trustees—ownership of property and even the right to have a say in naming pastors—but refused to concede to rebellious laity, egged on in many cases by rebellious priests, the power to choose and dismiss their pastors.

As the struggle persisted, there were schisms in New York, Philadelphia, Norfolk, and, before it was established as a diocese and England was appointed bishop, Charleston. Support was lent to trusteeism by a rationale that now seems highly esoteric but then struck not a few people as reasonable. As Catholic monarchs in Europe enjoyed the *Patronato Real*, or right of royal patronage, it was argued, so in the democratic United States the people should be recognized as possessing similar powers. Although the defenders of trusteeism engaged

---

[54] "The Period of Anglo-French Domination", in Fogarty, 2.

in pamphleteering and petitioned the Holy See, the response from Rome was unyielding, and in 1820 the new dioceses of Richmond and Charleston were created mainly so that there would be resident bishops on the spot, able to assess the challenge and meet it effectively.

Trusteeism was condemned at the First Provincial Council of Baltimore in 1829, largely at John England's urging, and the Patronato Real argument was formally rejected. In a pastoral letter directed to the Catholic laity, the bishops deplored the activities of those who, "not fully acquainted with the principles of our church government, either presumed to reform it upon the model of those who have separated from us, or claimed imaginary rights from the misapprehension of facts and laws with which they were badly, if at all acquainted". These laymen, they added, "have sometimes been abetted by ignorant or unprincipled priests; and disastrous schisms have thereby arisen".

The bishops' response was unequivocal: "[I]n no part of the Catholic Church does the right of instituting or dismissing a clergyman to or from any benefice or mission . . . exist in any one, save the ordinary prelate of the diocese or district in which such benefice or mission is found." The sole concession to the laity was an expression of hope that, in making clerical appointments, the bishops would "meet not only your wants but your wishes" insofar as they conscientiously could. That was all.[55]

Despite episcopal firmness, however, lay trusteeism persisted in one place or another during much of the century, springing up anew as other immigrant groups picked up where the Irish had left off. Wherever it appeared, it was rigorously condemned, and steps were taken to destroy it.

It hardly needs saying that trusteeism was an ugly business, inconsistent with Catholic ecclesiology and inimical to the unity of the community of Faith. Nevertheless its suppression,

[55] "Pastoral Letter to the Laity", Oct. 17, 1829, in Nolan, vol. 1, 45–46.

although necessary, carried with it certain negative consequences. The struggle against trusteeism, one historian says, was "a canonical, legal, and educational battle against an incipient Catholic congregationalism. Understandably, the campaign engendered in the American hierarchy a caution, sometimes even excessive, about delegating to laymen extensive authority over church temporalities."[56] Another writer says succinctly, "The condemnation of lay trusteeism . . . meant the end of an official lay voice in the church."[57]

This, then, was the state of things in the Church as it was reflected in the 1917 Code of Canon Law. It is hardly surprising that the ecclesiology underlying that document was thoroughly clericalist. For, at the time the Code was drafted, "there existed neither a theology of the laity nor any of the phenomena which, moved by the Holy Spirit, were to manifest themselves within the Church in eminently lay types of Christian life."[58] Hence a result not merely predictable but inevitable: "[T]he 1917 Code failed to pay adequate attention to the laity precisely because it would have been impossible for it to do so"; indeed, it paid "little attention to the rights and duties of the faithful as such", while the only provisions dealing specifically with laymen related to matrimonial law.[59]

Still, there were some signs of hope, if one only knew where to look for them. Even earlier, in fact, in the seventeenth and eighteenth centuries, a lay elite, reacting against the establishment of Protestantism in large parts of Europe and the "spread of unbelief and indifference" everywhere, had begun to turn its attention to "apostleship and defence of the Catholic faith by means other than those of the political powers".[60]

---

[56] R. F. McNamara, "Trusteeism", in *New Catholic Encyclopedia*, vol. 14 (Washington, D.C.: The Catholic University of America, 1967), 325.

[57] Fogarty, 3.

[58] Del Portillo, 11.

[59] Ibid., 10.

[60] Congar, 359.

One naturally thinks of a towering figure like Pascal, but there were others as well.

By the nineteenth century the impact of the Enlightenment, the progressive spread of cultural secularization, and the inroads of liberalism even within organized Christianity had begun to concentrate still more the energies of Catholic intellectuals, both clerical and lay. In certain circles there was a heightened awareness that an effective response to the crisis by the Church depended in large part upon the laity.

Congar writes, "Many priests and lay people appreciated the urgent necessity for making contact with this world, for finding ways of acting on it, for defending and explaining the faith in a language it could understand, for applying themselves to the Christian regeneration of society."[61] He cites names like Chateaubriand, de Maistre, and Montalembert to make his point. The spirit of it all was expressed by the Dominican preacher Lacordaire (1802–61): "The lay man has a mission to fulfil; he has to supply whatever may be lacking to the diocesan clergy and the religious orders, for their resources and for many means of action. Men of faith must join their efforts to defend truth against the ceaseless influence of evil teaching; their charity must work in common to repair the breaches in the Church and the social order."[62]

In time, this way of thinking reached the highest levels of the Church. Pope Leo XIII, in his 1890 encyclical *Sapientiae Christianae,* calls on laymen to cooperate actively with the clergy in teaching and spreading the Faith and urges organized lay action to meet social needs and challenges: "Let each one, therefore, bear in mind that he both can and should, so far as may be, preach the Catholic Faith by the authority of his example, and by open and constant profession of the obligations it imposes. . . . The faithful would not, however, so completely and advantageously satisfy these duties as is

[61] Ibid.
[62] Quoted in Congar, 360.

fitting they should were they to enter the field as isolated champions of the Faith."[63] The realization was growing that passivity on the part of the laity was unacceptable—for them, for the Church, and for the world.

In this way the stage was set for those great events of the early twentieth century that in our times have led to a veritable revolution, or perhaps renaissance, in the Church's official view of the laity and their relationship to the clergy. Among these perhaps the most important was the rise of Catholic Action.

Catholic Action was an important step forward in the Church's approach to laymen. Criticism of its limitations should not overlook that central fact. The movement was essentially an organized program of spiritual and intellectual formation for the laity, who then were expected to bring to bear their Catholic convictions and values upon the structures and institutions of secular society.

Despite occasional mockery (Catholic Action, a French quip had it, sought to remedy the incompetence [*l'insuffisance*] of the clergy by the impertinence [*la suffisance*] of the laity), the movement was on the right track in many ways. The systematic formation of laymen remains an urgent need, while the human and spiritual betterment of social institutions and structures was solemnly recognized by no less than Vatican Council II as the proper task, the specific apostolic responsibility, of the laity.

Yet Catholic Action was fundamentally flawed. The flaw lay in understanding lay apostolate as only the participation of the laity in the apostolate of the hierarchy and in the centralized clerical control and direction to which that naturally led. Thus Pope Pius XI, who to his lasting credit did

---

[63] In Etienne Gilson, ed., *The Church Speaks to the Modern World: The Social Teachings of Leo XIII* (New York: Doubleday Image Books, 1954), 257–58.

so much to initiate and promote Catholic Action: "[T]heir activity [i.e., the activity of laymen involved in Catholic Action] is a precious aid and necessary complement to the priestly ministry. And it is because of this consideration that since the beginning of our pontificate we have addressed to the hierarchy and to the people a paternal invitation that the faithful be properly prepared and organized in view of this apostolate which we defined [as] the participation of the laity in the hierarchical apostolate."[64]

Plainly this is an appropriate arrangement for some forms of lay activity. Certain lay ministries, for example, really are a form of participation by laymen in work proper to clerics, so it is right and necessary that they be directed and regulated by the clerical hierarchy. But by no means is this true of all lay activity of a religious nature.

Yet Catholic Action's basic mistake points to the conclusion that no form of Christian engagement belongs to laymen by right and all lay enterprises of an apostolic nature must be managed by the clergy. In fact, Catholic Action itself often was ingenuously described as the "long arm" of the hierarchy, enabling them to reach via the laity into regions where priests were unwelcome.

As we shall see, Vatican II set aside such notions. But even today it is fair to ask how many people "have really abandoned the narrow conception of the apostolate of the laity as a pastoral work *organized from the top down?* How many people have got beyond the previous 'monolithic' conception of the lay apostolate, and understand that it can and indeed should exist without the necessity of rigid centralized structures, canonical missions and hierarchical mandates?"[65]

---

[64] Apostolic Letter to the Hierarchy of the Philippines, in William Ferree, S. M., *Introduction to Catholic Action* (Washington, D.C.: National Catholic Welfare Conference, n.d.), 86.

[65] Josemaría Escrivá de Balaguer, *Conversations with Monsignor Escriva de Balaguer* (Mandaluyong, Metro Manila: Sinag-Tala Publishers, 1977), 32–33.

Even now in the United States it appears that most *organized* lay apostolate remains under at least de facto clerical control; perhaps that helps explain why there is, relatively speaking, so little of it.

Still, Catholic Action did play a crucial transitional role in the development of the Church's thinking about the laity. Its strengths and weaknesses alike are suggested in these words of Pope Pius XI:

> Catholic Action, we may say, is Catholic life, for just as there can be no action without life, neither can there be life without action. Catholic Action in effect aims at the formation of sincere Catholics, who will know, love and live the Christian life in its integrity, showing that it is possible to fulfill perfectly the duties which it imposes on all classes, in every social and professional sphere. . . . [T]he fate of Catholic Action lies in the hands of the clergy. . . . Catholic Action must by its very nature develop itself in the Diocese and be directly dependent on the Bishop, for, since Catholic Action is the participation of the laity in the apostolate of the Hierarchy, it is the Bishop who has the right, and also the duty, of establishing, organizing and directing Catholic Action in his own diocese.[66]

In its day it was very much. Now we know it was not—and *could not be*—enough. For the clericalist mentality, the lesson of Catholic Action is, or at least should be, clear: "All those who exercise the priestly ministry in the Church should always be careful to respect the autonomy which a Catholic layman needs, so that he will not find himself in a position of inferiority in relation to his fellow laymen, and can efficiently carry out his own apostolic task in the middle of the world."[67]

By no means was Catholic Action the only development in the first half of the twentieth century with a bearing upon

---

[66] Apostolic Letter to the Hierarchy of the Philippines, in Ferree, 86–88.
[67] Escrivá de Balaguer, 17.

the role of laymen and the clericalist mentality. Worthy of note, for example, are two encyclicals of Pope Pius XII, *Mystici Corporis* (1943) and *Mediator Dei* (1947).

As its title suggests, *Mystici Corporis* presents an ecclesiology based on the Pauline concept of the Church as the Mystical Body of Christ. In itself this is an important move away from the pyramidal, institutional model of the Church, toward what, especially since Vatican II, has come to be known as an ecclesiology of *communio* or "communion": the Church understood as a community of persons who are interactive and interdependent.

Of particular significance for our subject is the view of the laity taken by *Mystici Corporis*: although the Church, considered as a body, is hierarchically organized, she embraces diverse ministries, offices, and functions, and these constitute a structure within which laymen too, have roles. "Indeed, let this be clearly understood, especially in these our days: the fathers and mothers of families, and those who are spiritual parents through Baptism, and in particular those members of the laity who assist the ecclesiastical Hierarchy in spreading the Kingdom of the Divine Redeemer, occupy an honorable, even though often lowly place in the Christian community. Under the impulse of God and with his help they can reach the peak of holiness."[68] Moreover, according to Pope Pius, the laity have more to do than receive spiritual ministrations and be sanctified. For "Christ requires his members"; in fact, "the salvation of many" depends on their cooperative action. And all, including the laity, "have the obligation of working hard and constantly for the upbuilding and increase" of the Mystical Body; especially this is true of the members of Catholic Action.

Mediator Dei complements *Mystici Corporis* by discussing prayer and worship within the Mystical Body. Of special interest are its teaching on the priesthood of the faithful and

[68] *Mystici Corporis*, 23.

its emphasis on the essential distinction between the common priesthood and the ordained priesthood as both relate to the celebration of the Eucharist.

By reason of baptism, Pope Pius says, all the faithful "participate, according to their state, in the priesthood of Christ". This has particular relevance to the Mass. On the one hand, the holy sacrifice "is performed by the priest and by him alone as bearing the Person of Christ and not as taking the place of the faithful". On the other hand, the people have a share in this action

> in two ways; namely, they offer the sacrifice through the hands of the priest and, to a certain extent, they offer it together with him. . . . The people are said to offer sacrifice together with the priest not because the members of the Church perform the visible liturgical rite, as the priest does, who alone is divinely appointed for this function, but because they unite their prayers of praise, petition, expiation, and thanksgiving to the prayers and intention of the priest, and of the high priest himself, so that in the offering of the victim and in the external rite of the priest their prayers may be brought to the Father.[69]

Important practical developments preceded and accompanied these magisterial insights. These included the emergence and spread of the liturgical movement, with its emphasis on active lay participation in the Church's worship, and the appearance and growth of new lay groups such as Opus Dei, the secular institutes, and the Focolare movement, which stressed not only lay sanctity and lay apostolate but the autonomy of laymen in carrying out the specifically *ecclesial* mission that they receive in baptism and confirmation. Much of the new thinking was brought together in Yves Congar's *Lay People in the Church*, first published in 1951, which has been called a "veritable *Summa*" of the theology of the laity;[70] it contrib-

---

[69] In Clarkson et al., 299–300.   [70] Magnani, 585.

uted significantly to the rehabilitation of the laity. Under the inspiration of the Spirit, the Church in the decades leading up to the Second Vatican Council was striving earnestly, and often successfully, to reach a new and better understanding of laymen, their role, and their relationship to the clergy.

There is a great need for serious, scholarly historical studies of clericalism. Even from the preceding sketch, however, several broad conclusions emerge.

1. There were priests and laymen in the primitive Church (although these terms were not used to describe them), and the real differences between the two groups were recognized, especially in regard to their respective roles in the celebration of the Eucharist. *Sociological* differences were minimal, however. The clergy did *not* constitute a caste, and the laity were *not* viewed as naturally passive and subordinate to clerics. Emphasis was placed upon the unity and radical equality of all members of the community of Faith and upon the responsibility shared by all—though in diverse, complementary ways, according to their particular ministries, charisms, and offices—for carrying out the Church's mission.

2. In time, a process of clericalization set in. Distinctions, ever more sharply drawn, separated priests from laity, and the clerics grew ever more dominant within the community. This state of affairs was confirmed and extended under Constantine and his successors. The rise of monasticism and its assimilation of thinking about priestly spirituality in general also contributed to the process.

3. Despite lay investiture and the endless church-state struggles of the Middle Ages, the clericalist mentality played a central role during these centuries in determining thinking and practice about lay-clergy relationships in the Church.

4. Conditions produced by clericalism were part of the reality that the early Protestant Reformers assailed. The Catholic response, embodied in the Council of Trent, remedied many of the problems that had existed in the priest-

hood, but an unfortunate side effect of the Catholic reform movement was the further reinforcement it gave to clericalist thinking and practice.

5. Despite the clericalism prevailing in the Church in the eighteenth and nineteenth centuries, there were signs here and there of a growing awareness that the challenges posed by rationalism, religious liberalism, and secularization made it imperative for the Catholic laity to have a more active and effective religious role.

6. In the first half of the twentieth century, this awareness was crystalized in various new movements and new ways of thinking. The most visible response was the development of Catholic Action. It was a notable step forward in many respects, but it also contained built-in limitations arising from the view of lay apostolate as participation in the apostolate of the clerical hierarchy. Although this model is appropriate when applied to forms of lay activity (for example, certain lay ministries) that *are* a participation in clerical work, it does not recognize that laymen have an intrinsic duty, and a corresponding right, to engage in the apostolate arising from their reception of the sacraments of baptism and confirmation and requiring neither a hierarchical mandate nor clerical direction.

In this way the stage was set for Vatican Council II.

III

VATICAN II AND AFTER

Although it was not absolutely the first Church council at any level to deal substantively with the laity and their role, the Second Vatican Council was the first *ecumenical* council to do so—the first "to consider the question of the Church's understanding of itself in such a way as to give prominence or restore prominence in a positive sense to all the potential dignity of the laity to be found in revelation".[1] But it would be stretching a point to suggest that this was a council *about* the laity. Vatican II was "about" many things, and to understand its treatment of laymen and grasp what remains to be done in order to put it into effect, we must take a broad view of its underlying purposes.

That, nevertheless, is easier said than done. People who wish to coopt the Council for some ideology or cause typically describe it to their advantage, and that is a temptation to be resisted. In fact, Vatican II had a remarkably comprehensive agenda. Where to begin in identifying its purposes and measuring its achievement? With the reform of the liturgy, upon which its first document focuses and which probably remains for many Catholics its most visible result? With the many important doctrinal statements in the constitutions on the Church and on divine revelation, as well as several other

[1] Magnani, 593.

documents? With the impetus that it gave to new thinking about the priesthood and religious life? With its innovations regarding ecumenism and religious liberty? In these and other matters, Vatican II's work was of major importance.

In considering the Council's underlying purposes, however, we must start not with any of these but with the vision of Pope John XXIII. He had something definite in mind in convening the Council, and any evaluation of it and its aftermath, including the "new" position of the laity, must begin with that.

Though it was never a secret, what Pope John envisaged was and remains something so large and momentous that even today it is difficult to keep in focus. He wished to close the gap between the Church and the world and, analogously, between the natural and the supernatural in people's lives.

In the document formally convoking the Council in 1961,[2] Pope John speaks of a "crisis under way within society"—a crisis said to create for the Church a task of "immense gravity . . . as in the most tragic periods of its history". He explains: "It is a question in fact of bringing the modern world into contact with the vivifying and perennial energies of the gospel—a world which exalts itself with its conquests in the technical and scientific fields, but which brings also the consequences of a temporal order which some have wished to reorganize excluding God."

Pope John is here stating what he and most other observers would take to be a fundamental fact about the modern (or, today, postmodern) world: to a great extent it has lost sight of God. Whether or not particular individuals are believers, contemporary secular culture operates on the assumption either that God does not exist or else that he does not concern himself with human affairs, so that it is meaningless to say

[2] Apostolic Constitution *Humanae Salutis,* December 25, 1961, in Walter M. Abbott, S.J., and Gallagher, eds., *The Documents of Vatican II* (New York: Guild Press, 1966), 705–9.

individual lives and history as a whole ought to be directed to the conscious carrying-out of his providential plan. "Hence," the Pope says, "there is a weakening in the aspiration in the values of the spirit. Hence an urge for the almost exclusive search for earthly pleasures. . . . And hence there is a completely new and disconcerting fact: the existence of a militant atheism which is active on a world level."

Although it is still possible even in the late twentieth century to call this state of affairs new in some respects—against the background of two millennia of Christianity, after all, it truly *is* new—it did not emerge only in the decades immediately before 1961. The Church and secular culture in the West have been moving apart since at least the time of the Enlightenment and, arguably, much earlier than that. In fact, one might argue that the roots of this process, at least in part, go all the way back to the exaggerated otherworldliness, the all too literal *contemptus mundi,* expressed in various strains of Christian thinking that we have examined above.

In any case, and however far back the sundering of religion and culture might be traced, one obvious consequence over time was that the secular world more and more learned to view supernatural religion as irrelevant to, or even in conflict with, authentic human concerns, and as an obstacle to human progress. The natural result was secular humanism as we have experienced it in the twentieth century: militantly atheistic and messianic in its Marxist version, religiously indifferent and self-absorbed in the garb of Western consumerism.

There are many compelling accounts of the secularization of the West, but all paint essentially the same picture. Let Dietrich Bonhoeffer's summing-up stand for them all: "The movement that began about the thirteenth century . . . towards the autonomy of man . . . has in our time reached an undoubted completion. Man has learnt to deal with himself in all questions of importance without the 'working hypothesis' called 'God'. . . . As in the scientific field, so in human affairs generally, 'God' is being pushed more and more out of life, losing more and more ground."[3] But Bonhoeffer rejects an "attack by Christian apologetic on the adulthood of the world" as being pointless, ignoble, and un-Christian: "Pointless, because it seems to me like an attempt to put a grown-up man back into adolescence. . . . Ignoble, because it amounts to an attempt to exploit man's weakness for purposes that are alien to him and to which he has not freely assented. Unchristian, because it confuses Christ with one particular stage in man's religiousness."[4]

For Christians who agree with this analysis, it is clear that the solution to the problem lies in bringing "the adulthood of the world" and Christian Faith into harmony and practical integration. This was the approach adopted by Pope John. By midpoint in this century, he observed, Western secular culture, increasingly divorced from the influence of supernatural religion, was in rather desperate straits. Technological progress, combined with confusion and conflict over fundamental values, had brought humanity to the brink of an unprecedented crisis. And this paradoxically created an opportunity for the Church: "Many people who did not realize the importance of its mission in the past are, taught by experience, today more disposed to welcome its warnings."

Perhaps. But if the Church has nothing except warnings to address to the world, the world can be counted on to ignore her message. To Pope John's credit, he recognized this. Instead, he saw the Church as having an essentially positive role—one that, he maintained, she was in a good position to perform. Having weathered many tribulations during the last several centuries, she was by midpoint in this one a strong, healthy, self-confident community of Faith, "reinvigorated intellectually . . . interiorly purified . . . ready for trial". All that were needed were internal renewal and updating, in order to slough off those anachronistic cultural accretions

---

[3] *Letters and Papers from Prison* (New York: Macmillan, 1967), 167–68.
[4] Ibid., 169.

that still weighed down the Church and, in particular, to set aside definitively any lingering false ideas about the "world" that still kept the Church from playing the role in human affairs intended for her by God.

In broad brush strokes this is the background against which Vatican II's treatment of the Catholic laity should be understood. In this context it is easy to see that the Council's achievement was substantial.

The Second Vatican Council expresses at the highest levels of the hierarchical Church a commitment to Christian humanism and points to a new kind of Christian secularity with particular importance for the spirituality and apostolate of laymen. For example, the Pastoral Constitution on the Church in the Modern World declares the object of the Council's attention to be "the world of men, the whole human family along with the sum of those realities in the midst of which that family lives".[5] Yet the Council does not succumb to the temptation to initiate a simplistic adaptation, or accommodation, of the Church to the world. Fundamentally, of course, this is out of respect for the Church's nature, but it also partly reflects a recognition of the human condition as it is. The world has been "emancipated" by Christ, but this emancipation was itself necessary only because the world had fallen into "the bondage of sin", whose ugly consequences persist even in the face of Christ's redemptive act.[6]

In view of this central reality of the world and the human condition, the Council undertakes to show its solidarity with the human family by entering into dialogue with it concerning its problems. In sum:

> This sacred Synod proclaims the highest destiny of man and champions the godlike seed which has been sown in him. It offers to mankind the honest assistance of the Church in fostering that brotherhood of all men which corresponds to this

[5] *Gaudium et Spes*, 2.   [6] Ibid.

destiny of theirs. Inspired by no earthly ambition, the Church
seeks but a solitary goal: to carry forward the work of Christ
Himself under the lead of the befriending Spirit. And Christ
entered this world to give witness to the truth, to rescue
and not to sit in judgment, to serve and not to be served.[7]

It is a magnificent vision.

On the one hand, Vatican II does not make the mistake
of understanding human fulfillment only in temporal terms.
The human fulfillment with which the Church ultimately is
concerned is the fulfillment to be realized in heaven. On the
other hand, rejecting the excesses of extreme otherworldliness,
the Council underlines the *continuity* between life in this world
and life in the next, a continuity embodied in the reality
called "the kingdom". We shall see later the profound implications
that this has for our subject. Furthermore, in the Council's
view this continuity has immediate consequences for
the question of vocation as well as for the significance of
human temporal activity and apostolate in and to the secular
order. As *Gaudium et Spes* points out, "The gifts of the Spirit
are diverse. He calls some to give clear witness to the desire
for a heavenly home and to keep that desire green among
the human family. He summons others to dedicate themselves
to the earthly service of men and to make ready the material
for the celestial realm by this ministry."[8]

Thus Vatican II's dominant theme is positive engagement
between Christians and their temporal surroundings—the
world. Even the profession of religious vows, it says, serves
the purpose of offering testimony to men in the world concerning
eschatological realities.[9] The Council calls on Christians
"as citizens of two cities" to "strive to discharge their
earthly duties conscientiously and in response to the gospel
spirit". For "they are mistaken who, knowing that we have
here no abiding city but seek one which is to come, think

[7] Ibid., 3.
[8] Ibid., 38.
[9] See *Lumen Gentium,* 44.

that they may therefore shirk their earthly responsibilities." Nor is any encouragement offered to those who might imagine they can satisfy their religious obligations "by acts of worship alone and in the discharge of certain moral obligations", while at the same time approaching temporal affairs as if they were "altogether divorced from the religious life". Vatican II declares emphatically that "this split between the faith which many profess and their daily lives deserves to be counted among the more serious errors of our age."[10]

This, then, is the setting of the Second Vatican Council's charter for the laity. It is of more than symbolic significance that this charter is found mainly in the Council's central document, the Dogmatic Constitution on the Church, *Lumen Gentium:* for its view of the laity, the Council wishes us to understand, is rooted not in sociological factors but in the Church's very nature. In *Lumen Gentium,* together with the Decree on the Apostolate of the Laity, *Apostolicam Actuositatem,* which adds details to the ecclesiological vision of the other document, laymen are said to have a role of critical importance in the Church's mission—a role, moreover, that is intrinsically theirs, theirs by obligation and by right, inasmuch as they have been baptized and confirmed.

To be sure, "the laity can . . . be called in various ways to a more direct form of cooperation in the apostolate of the hierarchy."[11] Thus the assumption underlying Catholic Action in its day was correct (as far as it went), just as that same assumption is correct (as far as it goes) in the case of certain lay ministries today: laymen can and sometimes do participate in the work of the clerical hierarchy. But that is not the most important fact about the laity and their role. Rather, "The lay apostolate . . . is a participation in the saving mission of the Church itself. Through their baptism and confirmation, all are commissioned to that apostolate

---

[10] *Gaudium et Spes*, 43.   [11] *Lumen Gentium*, 33.

by the Lord Himself."[12] Laymen therefore do not have an option—to take part in the apostolate or not to take part, as suits them. Having been baptized and confirmed, they are "strictly obliged to spread and defend the faith both by word and by deed".[13]

Most important of all, the Council's "universal call to holiness" is directed to the laity as much as it is to clerics and religious. There is no suggestion here that the lay state is a compromise to accommodate the weakness of people who lack the generosity to enter the priesthood or religious life and who, even if they do manage to save their souls, cannot aspire to heroic sanctity. On the contrary, "it is evident to everyone that all the faithful of Christ of whatever rank or status are called to the fullness of the Christian life and to the perfection of charity."[14] The Council particularly, though not exclusively, mentions married couples, parents, and workers. It is essential that the laity, like clerical and religious *christifideles,* interpret their situations in vocational terms and respond accordingly: "All of Christ's faithful . . . whatever be the conditions, duties, and circumstances of their lives, will grow in holiness day by day through these very situations, if they accept all of them with faith from the hand of their heavenly Father."[15]

In the thinking of Vatican II there is also another central fact about the laity: secularity. The Council makes this point in a number of places. For example: "A secular quality is proper and special to laymen."[16] "Secular duties and activities belong properly although not exclusively to laymen."[17] Sanctity itself is to be achieved by the laity *in the world,* through the performance of their secular duties. Their secularity is both a sociological and a theological fact, and it radically

[12] Ibid.
[13] Ibid.
[14] Ibid., 40.
[15] Ibid., 41.
[16] Ibid., 30.
[17] *Gaudium et Spes,* 43.

determines the nature of the apostolate proper to them: i.e., they "are called in a special way to make the Church present and operative in those places and circumstances where only through them can she become the salt of the earth".[18] Practically speaking, this means apostolate by laymen carried on in and to the world: "The laity must take on the renewal of the temporal order as their own special obligation."[19]

Indeed, secularity is precisely the distinguishing characteristic of the *ecclesial* role of laymen. The laity, the Constitution on the Church points out, "are in their own way made sharers in the priestly, prophetic, and kingly functions of Christ. They carry out their own part in the mission of the whole Christian people with respect to the Church and the world."[20] This is to say,

> the laity, by their very vocation, seek the kingdom of God by engaging in temporal affairs and by ordering them according to the plan of God. They live in the world, that is, in each and in all of the secular professions and occupations. They live in the ordinary circumstances of family and social life, from which the very web of their existence is woven.
>
> They are called there by God so that by exercising their proper function and being led by the spirit of the gospel they can work for the sanctification of the world from within, in the manner of leaven.[21]

It is within this context that the Council revives and develops the idea of the priesthood of the faithful arising from baptism. While stressing the essential difference between ordained and nonordained priesthood,[22] it also emphasizes that each "in its own special way" is "a participation in the one priesthood of Christ". Thus, "The ministerial priest, by the sacred power he enjoys, molds and rules the priestly people. Acting in the person of Christ, he brings about the Eucharistic

---

[18] Ibid., 33.
[19] *Apostolicam Actuoisitatem*, 7.
[20] *Lumen Gentium*, 31.
[21] Ibid.
[22] Ibid., 10.

Sacrifice, and offers it to God in the name of all the people. For their part, the faithful join in the offering of the Eucharist by virtue of their royal priesthood. They likewise exercise that priesthood by receiving the sacraments, by prayer and thanksgiving, by the witness of a holy life, and by self-denial and active charity."[23]

Once again, the Council goes out of its way to emphasize that this priestly role belongs to lay people, to whom Christ gives "a share in His priestly function of offering spiritual worship for the glory of God and the salvation of men".[24]

> For all their works, prayers, and apostolic endeavors, their ordinary married and family life, their daily labor, their mental and physical relaxation, if carried out in the Spirit, and even the hardships of life, if patiently borne—all of these become spiritual sacrifices acceptable to God through Jesus Christ (cf. 1 Pet 2:5). During the celebration of the Eucharist, these sacrifices are most lovingly offered to the Father along with the Lord's body. Thus, as worshipers whose every deed is holy, the laity consecrate the world itself to God.[25]

The laity, then, are called by God to exercise their special participation in Christ's priesthood precisely through service in and to the world and the *consecratio mundi* that they accomplish by the apostolically motivated performance of their secular duties. It is their faithful commitment to these purposes that, above all, they bring with them to the celebration of the Eucharist, in order to be offered there, through the ministry of the ordained priest, in union with the committed self-offering of Christ.

Catholic laymen by right enjoy real autonomy in their apostolate in and to the secular order. They are not the agents, the long arm, of bishops and priests. To be sure, when the hierarchy "entrusts to the laity some functions which are

---

[23] Ibid.
[24] Ibid., 34.
[25] Ibid.

more closely connected with pastoral duties, such as the teaching of Christian doctrine, certain liturgical actions, and the care of souls"—when, as we would now say, the laity are commissioned to engage in lay ministries—they are "fully subject to higher ecclesiastical direction in the performance of such work".[26] But this is *not* the case when, either individually or collectively, they seek to do Christ's work in the world, making no claim to be official, mandated representatives of the hierarchy: "The laity must take on the renewal of the temporal order as their own special obligation. Led by the light of the gospel and the mind of the Church, and motivated by Christian love, let them act directly and definitively in the temporal sphere. As citizens they must cooperate with other citizens, using their own particular skills and acting on their own responsibility."[27]

In sum, Vatican II was the first ecumenical council to deal specifically and at length with the role of the laity and to do so in a positive manner. Its view of the laity includes an appreciation of the serious obligations, as well as the dignity, belonging to them by reason of their status as members, with their clergy, of Christ's faithful, the *christifideles*. It would be difficult to exaggerate the importance of the Council's contribution to the overcoming of clericalism and the advancement of laymen.

But the Council did not answer every conceivable question about the nature and role of the laity. For example, while affirming the essential difference between the ordained priesthood and the baptismal priesthood, Vatican II does not spend much time spelling out its nature.

Is it then sufficient to locate the difference, as sometimes is done, in the power possessed only by ordained priests to offer Mass and give absolution? Perhaps so. Yet this seems to restrict ordained ministry in a way that, for better or worse,

---

[26] *Apostolicam Actuositatem*, 24.   [27] Ibid., 7; cf. *Gaudium et Spes*, 43.

many men today apparently think makes it insufficiently rewarding to attract them to the priesthood or hold their interest if they do become priests. The problem is often said to be further aggravated by the spread of lay ministries that assign laymen nonsacramental functions previously reserved to clerics. Although this is a positive and desirable development in its own right, it apparently contributes to the contemporary identity crisis of priests. One looks in vain to Vatican II for definitive clarification of these issues, which the Council evidently did not anticipate but which now are sources of confusion for many lay and clerical Catholics.

Again, the Council documents are not very helpful in determining the relative importance of lay ministries in the Church on the one hand and lay apostolate in the world on the other. No doubt rightly, Vatican II has kind words to say about both. Since the Council, however, the impression often has been created that genuinely committed laymen not only may but also should express their commitment through "ministry"—that is, in Church work of some sort. The fact that apostolate in and to the secular order *is* the ecclesial work proper to the laity has very often been ignored. It is symptomatic of this that, although many programs of education and formation are now available to laymen preparing for ministry, systematic formation of the laity to undertake their secular duties in the spirit of apostolate is almost totally lacking.

At an even deeper level, still another unresolved issue—central to Vatican II—has enormous impact upon the Church's understanding of laymen and their understanding of themselves. It concerns the assumption, largely unexamined up to now, that returning to the roots of Catholic Christianity, as the Council intended, can only lead to a positive relationship between the Church and the world.

Recall that through the eighteenth, nineteenth, and twentieth centuries the Church, before Vatican II, more and more had raised her ramparts against a secular culture that she generally perceived as not just alien but also hostile. In this way the Church became less and less able to influence that culture for the better. The crucial work of culture formation instead was surrendered to the proponents and spokesmen of a de-Christianized secularity.

It did not necessarily follow, however, that simply tearing down the ramparts would at once produce happy results. This was especially unlikely to happen if Catholics—clerics, religious, and laity alike—were inadequately prepared for an unmediated encounter with the secular culture. To a great extent, of course, precisely that happened: the project of tearing down ramparts proceeded apace during and after the Council, little was done to prepare the Church's members for the consequences, and the results during the last thirty years have been—to put it as neutrally as possible—mixed. The ensuing tension between traditional Christianity and contemporary secularity today manifests itself not just intellectually but also in the lived experience of countless Catholics; it helps explain much of the postconciliar distress of the Church.

In the years since Vatican II, nevertheless, Church leaders have taken some important steps to carry out the implications of its ecclesiology, including that ecclesiology's implications for laymen. The revised Code of Canon Law, published in 1983, is a major instance.

Taking for granted Vatican II's vision of the Church as a *communio* or community, the Code seeks to express this in juridical terms. As one canonist remarks, "Although the canons refer to three groups of the faithful—clergy, laity, and religious—these share a true spiritual equality based on their baptism. . . . The question is not one of superiority, but of diversity among the people of God, diversity of members, gifts, and functions united in the Spirit for the building up of the Body of Christ."[28] Thus the 1983 Code recognizes many important obligations and rights belonging to laymen precisely in their capacity as full members, along with clerics and religious, of "Christ's faithful".

Even so, it is possible to find discordant views concerning the Code's treatment of laymen. One author, discussing Canon 207 (the last of four canons introducing Book II, "The People of God"), professes to be "greatly disturbed by interpretations that apparently tend to go too far in reducing the basic and fundamental *communio* to a *communio hierarchica* that seems to emphasize the *hierarchica* aspect unduly".[29]

At least with respect to Canon 207 itself, however, this concern appears unwarranted. The text reads in part as follows: "By divine institution, among Christ's faithful there are in the Church sacred ministers, who in law are also called clerics; the others are called lay people." But this hierarchical division of the Church into two large groups should be read in the context of other canons describing the Church and her structure—for example, Canon 204.1: "Christ's faithful are those who, since they are incorporated into Christ through baptism, are constituted the people of God. For this reason they participate in their own way in the priestly, prophetic and kingly office of Christ. They are called, each according to his or her particular condition, to exercise the mission which God entrusted to the Church to fulfill in the world." Clearly grounded in the doctrine of Vatican II, this affirmation recognizes the unity and equality of the Church's members as firmly and explicitly as anyone could ask. In this light there are no reasonable grounds for objecting to Canon 207's complementary affirmation that the community of Faith is hierarchically structured, and indeed that its hierarchical structure is "by divine institution". To reject this view would

---

[28] Thomas P. Doyle, O.P., *Rights and Responsibilities: A Catholic's Guide to the New Code of Canon Law* (New York: Pueblo Publishing Company, 1983), 8–9.

[29] Magnani, 620.

mean rejecting the ecclesiological understanding that the Catholic Church has of herself in the belief that it represents the will of her Divine Founder.

Nevertheless, underlying such expressions of concern we can discern a real issue of great importance. It has to do with an unresolved—and perhaps, in the nature of things, unresolvable—tension.

The hierachical division into clergy and laity expressed in Canon 207.1 is of the essence of the Church, but it does not exhaust the reality of the Church. It exists alongside the radical unity and equality of the *christifideles,* arising from baptism, which Canon 204.1 affirms no less clearly. The problem this presents is obvious: How shall we respect and uphold *both* principles—hierarchical structure and all it implies about authority and offices on the one hand, unity and radical equality of all Christ's faithful on the other—while resisting the temptation to exaggerate or downplay either? This is a difficult challenge.

Moreover, the emphases embodied in these two canons correspond, respectively, to the attitudes of clericalism on the one hand and neocongregationalism on the other. This is *not* to say that the Code of Canon Law itself encourages either; on the contrary, the Code plainly does not intend that either of its complementary ecclesiological principles should be understood and acted upon apart from the other. But the difficulty with complementary principles is how to keep them in balance; always the strong temptation exists to emphasize one at the other's expense. So, it can be argued, depending upon which of these canons one chooses to highlight, it is possible to find—out of context, to be sure—juridical support for the principle underlying either clericalism or neocongregationalism.

Corresponding to each principle, moreover, is a particular understanding of vocation. The ecclesiological emphasis of Canon 207.1 upon the Church's division into two broad classes of persons, clerics and laymen, roughly corresponds to the idea of vocation as state in life. But the clericalist mentality, as we have seen earlier, takes the vocation to the clerical state to be the ideal standard for all—the only *real* vocation, as it were—and this lends support to the idea that the clergy naturally are meant to dominate and direct a passive, subservient laity. As for the emphasis on unity and radical equality mirrored in Canon 204.1 (and others: for example, Canon 208, which speaks of the "genuine equality of dignity and action among all Christ's faithful" flowing from "their rebirth in Christ"), it corresponds—if taken in isolation and not linked, as it should be, to the complementary principle of hierarchical structure—to neocongregationalism's exaggerated emphasis on the baptismal vocation common to all.

All this points to a conclusion. Not just in Canon Law but in the life of the Church and the lives of Christ's faithful, a principle of synthesis is needed to bring these diverse understandings of vocation, and the discordant patterns of ecclesiological structuring to which they individually correspond, into a dynamic relationship of harmonious complementarity.

Such a principle exists. It is the understanding of vocation as the unique calling that each person receives from God to participate in the mission of Christ and the Church's mission in his own irreducibly individual manner. Here and there the 1983 Code seems to hint at something like this: e.g., Canon 208: "They all contribute, each according to *his or her own condition and office* [emphasis added], to the building up of the Body of Christ"; Canon 210: "All Christ's faithful, each according to *his or her own condition* [emphasis added], must make a wholehearted effort to lead a holy life." But the Code does not develop the idea. As we shall see, it has become urgent to do so.

There have been other milestones along the way since Vatican Council II. One of these was the Extraordinary Synod of Bishops convened by Pope John Paul in 1985 to evaluate the Council's implementation and the state of the Church twenty years after its conclusion. Several of its themes are important for our subject.

Before the event, some journalistic speculations, apparently fueled by people with no great fondness for the Pope and his collaborators, had asked whether the Synod, acting at the Pope's instigation, was preparing to repudiate the Council.[30] The question was profoundly misplaced. The great debate in the Church today is not about whether to embrace Vatican II or spurn it but over how the Council should be interpreted so as to continue shaping the Church in its light. People at both extremes of the ideological spectrum would gladly set aside Vatican II—those on the far right in order to return to some preconciliar golden age, those on the far left in order to "democratize" the Church and relativize her doctrine in ways quite unrelated to the Council; but for the vast majority the argument concerns what Vatican II really meant and how to continue its work.

This was clear from the Final Report of the 1985 Synod. "Unanimously", the bishops declared, "we have celebrated the Second Vatican Council as a grace of God and a gift of the Holy Spirit, from which have come forth many spiritual fruits for the universal Church and the particular churches, as well as for the men of our time. Unanimously and joyfully, we also verify that the council is a legitimate and valid expression and interpretation of the deposit of faith as it is found in sacred Scripture and in the living tradition of the Church."[31] So much for scare-mongering.

Reasonably enough, however, the Synod offered corrective

---

[30] I recall an incident in Rome shortly before the Synod began. Two American reporters approached me to check out the rumor that Cardinal Joseph Ratzinger, Prefect of the Congregation for the Doctrine of the Faith, had once been a committed Nazi. Upon learning that the Cardinal was twelve years old when World War II broke out, they went away disappointed.

[31] *A Message to the People of God and the Final Report* (Washington, D.C.: National Conference of Catholic Bishops, 1986), 9.

guidance on some important matters. The euphoria of the 1960s had long since vanished and been replaced by a more realistic assessment of the obstacles to renewing the Church and accomplishing her positive engagement with the secular world. Among the "internal causes" of difficulties the bishops noted a "partial and selective reading of the council" as well as "a superficial interpretation of its doctrine". The solution, they held, lay in "a deeper reception of the council", proceeding in four successive phases: "a deeper and more extensive knowledge of the council, its interior assimilation, its loving reaffirmation, and its implementation".[32]

As for external causes of the situation, the Synod took note of the Church's lack of "material means and personnel" in many places and the restrictions forcibly imposed on her in some. In the First World, moreover, the bishops found far less openness to religious influence than many Church people optimistically had expected twenty years earlier: "In the wealthy nations, we see the constant growth of an ideology characterized by pride in technical advances and a certain immanentism that leads to the idolatry of material goods (so-called consumerism). From this can follow . . . blindness to spiritual realities and values. In addition, we cannot deny the existence in society of forces capable of great influence which act with a certain hostile spirit toward the Church."[33] In sum; "all of these things manifest the work of the 'prince of this world' and of the 'mystery of iniquity' even in our day."

This points to an inescapable conclusion: "It seems to us that . . . God wishes to teach us more deeply the value, the importance, and the centrality of the cross of Jesus Christ." This is a reason not for abandoning the Council's program of renewal but for approaching it realistically.

> From this paschal perspective, which affirms the unity of the cross and the resurrection, the true and false meaning of

[32] Ibid., 11.   [33] Ibid., 10.

so-called *aggiornamento* is discovered. An easy accommodation that could lead to the secularization of the Church is to be excluded. Also excluded is an immobile closing in upon itself of the community of the faithful. Affirmed instead is a missionary openness for the integral salvation of the world. Through this, all truly human values not only are accepted but energetically defended: the dignity of the human person, fundamental human rights, peace, freedom from oppression, poverty, and injustice. But integral salvation is obtained only if these human realities are purified and further elevated, through grace, to human familiarity with God, through Jesus Christ in the Holy Spirit.[34]

This vision of the Church and the world is crucial to situating the Catholic laity correctly and understanding their role. Laymen, the 1985 Synod observed, "must perform their role in the Church in their daily occupations, such as the family, the workplace, secular activities, and leisure time, so as to permeate and transform the world with the light and life of Christ".[35] This assumes that the world as it is *can* be so permeated and transformed; it also assumes that the world as it is *stands in need* of the gospel's transforming influence.

Appropriately, the theme of the next ordinary assembly of the Synod, in 1987, was "The Vocation and Mission of the Laity in the Church and in the World Twenty Years after the Second Vatican Council". Preceded by "a greater degree of preparation and consultation than any other [synod assembly] to date",[36] the gathering brought together 232 bishops and other clerical participants, along with 60 mainly lay auditors, for a month-long discussion.

Its most concrete and lasting product was Pope John Paul's apostolic exhortation *Christifideles Laici,* dated December 30, 1988, the feast of the Holy Family, and released January 30,

---

[34] Ibid., 22.

[35] Ibid., 14.

[36] Msgr. Peter Coughlan, *The Hour of the Laity* (Philadelphia: E. J. Dwyer, 1989), 3.

1989. We shall return frequently to this important document. Here let us begin with an overview of what it says. This is all the more necessary because U.S. media largely ignored both the Pope's document and the Synod itself, apparently judging the latter's "safe" theme lacking in the element of controversy that makes for news. (The little coverage that the event received tended to focus on women's ordination and "altar girls"—issues whose relationship to the concerns of a Synod on the laity seems tenuous at best.) Nevertheless, *Christifideles Laici* is the most important treatment of the role of Catholic laymen to appear since Vatican II and is likely to remain so for years to come.

The apostolic exhortation begins by praising the progress since the Council in involving the laity in the Church's mission. John Paul points to "the new manner of active collaboration among priests, religious and the lay faithful; the active participation in the liturgy, in the proclamation of the word of God and catechesis; the multiplicity of services and tasks entrusted to the lay faithful and fulfilled by them; the flourishing of groups, associations and spiritual movements as well as a lay commitment in the life of the Church; and the fuller and meaningful participation of women in the development of society" (2). All that is to the good; but there are also problems. Two in particular stand out: overemphasis on "church services and tasks" at the expense of the laity's vocation in and to the world and "separation of faith from life".

The Pope states the overriding aim of the Synod in these words: that Catholic laymen "take an active, conscientious and responsible part in the mission of the Church in this great moment of history" (3). He characterizes the dark side of this historical moment by citing three disturbing phenomena: secularism, violations of human dignity, and the many forms of conflict, violence, terrorism, and war.

Even so, humanity has reason for hope. The fundamental reason is Jesus Christ and the good news of redemption:

"The lay faithful have an essential and irreplaceable role in this announcement and in this testimony: through them the Church of Christ is made present in the various sectors of the world as a sign and source of hope and love" (7).

Pope John Paul stresses that the lay vocation does not come by delegation. Arising from the sacraments of baptism and confirmation, it belongs to laymen by the very fact that they are members of the Church: "The participation of the lay faithful in the threefold mission of Christ as Priest, Prophet and King finds its source in the anointing of Baptism, its further development in Confirmation, and its realization and dynamic sustenance in the Holy Eucharist" (14).

But what specifically distinguishes laymen from priests and religious? Citing Vatican II, the Pope says it is their "secular character" (15). That the laity live and work in the world is not only a sociological fact but also "a theological and ecclesiological reality"—for, in the Council's language, laymen are "seeking the kingdom of God by engaging in temporal affairs and by ordering them to the plan of God".

They also are called to be saints. The Council spoke of the universal call to holiness, and Pope John Paul makes its message his own: "On an equal par with all other members of the Church, the lay faithful are called to holiness" (16). Moreover, in keeping with their secular character and vocation, they are meant to manifest their commitment to "life according to the Spirit . . . in their involvement in temporal affairs and in their participation in earthly activities" (17).

Turning to the question of laymen *in the Church,* the Pope begins by emphasizing the Vatican II ecclesiology of communion. This is expressed in the image of the Church as the Mystical Body of Christ. It follows that "every member of the lay faithful is seen in relation to the whole body and offers a totally unique contribution on behalf of the whole body" (20). The "ministries and charisms" of laymen are practical expressions of this. Although ordained ministries have a "primary position", with the approval of the authorities the laity too can have ministries, offices, and roles in the Church and can exercise their charisms or spiritual gifts in the Church's service, provided these are validated by the Church's pastors (21–22).

Positive as all this is, certain problems identified by the Synod also must be kept in mind: "a too-indiscriminate use of the word 'ministry', the confusion and the equating of the common priesthood and the ministerial priesthood, the lack of observance of ecclesiastical laws and norms, the arbitrary interpretation of the concept of 'supply', the tendency towards a 'clericalization' of the lay faithful and the risk of creating, in reality, an ecclesial structure of parallel service to that founded on the Sacrament of Orders" (23).

The principles relevant to the participation of laymen in the Church apply at all levels, but for most of the laity the parish is the "most immediate and visible expression" of the Church: it is the community of Faith where their Christian lives are nurtured and grow (26). Hence the importance of parish renewal: "The lay faithful ought ever more to be convinced of the special meaning that their commitment to the apostolate takes on in their parish" (27).

While stressing the "absolute necessity" of the apostolic activity of each individual member of the Church—each, after all, has been "entrusted with a unique task which cannot be done by another and which is to be fulfilled for the good of all" (28)—the Pope also speaks with approval of "associations, groups, communities, movements" for the laity, noting that "in modern times such lay groups have received a special stimulus" (29). Laymen have "a true and proper right" to form such groups, a right not based upon any "concession" by clerical authority but rooted in their baptism. Still, it is essential to evaluate all such groups by the "criteria of ecclesiality": commitment to the universal call to holiness, doctrinal fidelity, loyalty to the Pope and bishops, conformity to the Church's apostolic goals, and determination to be a true Christian "presence" in society (30).

Christifideles Laici turns next to the "coresponsibility" of the laity for carrying on the mission of the Church: "The lay faithful, precisely because they are members of the Church, have the vocation and mission of proclaiming the Gospel: they are prepared for this work by the sacraments of Christian initiation and by the gifts of the Holy Spirit" (33). Moreover, "every disciple is personally called by name; no disciple can withhold making a response: 'Woe to me if I do not preach the gospel' (1 Cor 9:16)."

Pope John Paul discusses the mission of evangelization at length, especially the need for what he calls, here and in many other places, "reevangelization" in the traditionally Christian, but now largely secularized, nations of the West: "Whole countries and nations, where religion and the Christian life were formerly flourishing and capable of fostering a viable and working community of faith, are now put to a hard test and, in some cases, are even undergoing a radical transformation as a result of a constant spreading of an indifference to religion, of secularism and atheism. This particularly concerns countries and nations of the so-called First World, in which economic well-being and consumerism . . . inspire and sustain a life lived 'as if God did not exist' " (34).

This points to an obvious task for the laity: "Their responsibility, in particular, is to testify how the Christian faith constitutes the only fully valid response . . . to the problems and hopes that life poses to every person and society. This will be possible if the lay faithful will know how to overcome in themselves the separation of the Gospel from life, again to take up in their daily activities in family, work and society, an integrated approach to life that is fully brought about by the inspiration and strength of the Gospel."

John Paul cites eight areas especially in need of the attention of Catholic laymen today.

1. Promoting the dignity and rights of the human person. "The dignity of the person constitutes the foundation of the

equality of all people among themselves. As a result, all forms of discrimination are totally unacceptable" (37).

2. Fostering respect for life. This is a task especially for parents, teachers, health workers, and people with "economic and political power" (38).

3. Supporting religious liberty and respect for the rights of conscience (39).

4. Assisting marriage and family life: "The family can and must require from all, beginning with public authority, the respect for those rights which, in saving the family, will save society itself" (40).

5. Carrying on the works of charity, i.e., "contemporary forms of the traditional spiritual and corporal works of mercy" (41).

6. Serving in public life. Despite criticism of politics and politicians, the Pope insists, there is no excuse for "either scepticism or an absence on the part of Christians in public life" (42).

7. Promoting social and economic justice. Economic structures must serve persons, not vice versa; in particular, laymen should strive to make justice and respect for human dignity operative in work and the workplace (43).

8. Engaging in the evangelization of culture: "The Church calls upon the lay faithful to be present in the privileged places of culture, that is, the world of education—school and university—in places of scientific and technological research, the areas of artistic creativity and work in the humanities" (44).

Next *Christifideles Laici* takes up various categories of the laity, styled "laborers in the Lord's vineyard". Here John Paul gives particular attention to young people and children (46–47), older people (48), and women.

As Pope John XXIII pointed out a quarter of a century earlier, the growing consciousness of women's dignity and their entry into public life are authentic "signs of the times" in our day. Although, in fidelity to Christ's will, it is not possible for the Church to ordain women to the priesthood, nevertheless "it is quite clear from the words and attitude of Christ, that no discrimination exists on the level of an individual relation to Christ, and on the level of participation in the Church's life of grace and holiness" (50).

As for women and the apostolate, "in speaking about participation in the apostolic mission of the Church, there is no doubt that in virtue of Baptism and Confirmation, a woman—as well as a man—is made a sharer in the three-fold mission of Jesus Christ, Priest, Prophet and King, and is thereby charged and given the ability to fulfill the fundamental apostolate of the Church: evangelization" (51). Women must do this by using their special gifts and talents. The document speaks of "two great tasks in particular . . . bringing full dignity to the conjugal life and to motherhood" (which, the Pope suggests, is a powerful way of evangelizing men) and "assuring the moral dimension of culture" (51).

And men? The Pope recalls that during the Synod "many voices were raised" expressing concern lest too much emphasis on women deepen an already existing problem, namely, the "absence or scarcity" of men engaged in apostolic and religious activities. Among common areas of male neglect cited by John Paul are "participation in the liturgical prayer of the Church, education and, in particular, catechesis of their own sons and daughters and other children, presence at religious and cultural meetings, and collaboration in charitable and missionary initiatives" (52).

To respond to a challenge of this magnitude, laymen evidently need formation; indeed, the Pope maintains that a "total and ongoing formation" of the laity should be among the priorities of every diocese (57). Its primary purpose should be to help people recognize and accept their personal vocations. Its elements include "a receptive listening to the word of God and the Church, fervent and constant prayer, recourse to a wise and loving spiritual guide, and a faithful discernment of the gifts and talents given by God as well as the diverse social and historic situations in which one lives" (58).

Formation also must reflect and emphasize the special nature of the laity's calling to be committed Christians in the secular world: "There cannot be two parallel lives in their existence: on the one hand, the so-called 'spiritual' life, with its values and demands; and on the other, the so-called 'secular' life. Every activity, every situation, every precise responsibility—as, for example, skill and solidarity in work, love and dedication in the family and the education of children, service to society and public life and the promotion of truth in the area of culture—are the occasions ordained by providence for a 'continuous exercise of faith, hope and charity'" (59).

John Paul lists the elements of a formation program for the laity as spiritual, doctrinal (especially social doctrine), and the cultivation of human talents and professional skills (60). Its instruments include the teaching office of the Pope and bishops; the parish, including small intraparochial communities; the family; Catholic schools; colleges and universities; and lay groups, associations, and movements of all kinds (61–62).

Christifideles Laici concludes with an appeal and a prayer. The appeal comes down to this: "The whole Church, pastors and lay faithful alike, standing on the threshold of the third millennium, ought to feel strongly the Church's responsibility to obey the command of Christ, 'Go into all the world and preach the Gospel to the whole of creation.'" The prayer, as so often in the writings of John Paul II, invokes the intercession of Mary: "Enable us to do our part in helping to establish on earth the civilization of truth and love, as God wills it, for His glory" (64).

An impressive document in many ways.

Is this then a story with a happy ending—clericalism vanquished in a blaze of conciliar and postconciliar insights?

Not really.

Appearing a quarter of a century after Vatican Council II, *Christifideles Laici* sets out an ideal that is still not widely understood and practiced. The current condition of the Catholic laity in the United States—always making allowance for the many positive exceptions—is marked by widespread apathy, alienation, and rebellion. Even active and committed laymen frequently carry the burden of their own clericalist attitudes as well as those of other Catholics. The clericalism involved may be either the old-fashioned, paternalistic clerical elitism or the new, well-intentioned but mistaken notion that the laity's advancement comes about by permitting them to do work previously reserved for priests. All too often, this latter approach has the effect of clericalizing the committed laity while further alienating the mass of laymen who have no intention of becoming involved in ministries and no idea that it is they, not priests and religious, whom God mainly calls to continue Jesus' work in the world.

Next we must examine all these problems at close range.

IV

PROBLEMS OF THE PRESENT MOMENT

More than a year and a half before the Synod of 1987, the Vatican sent the world's bishops a questionnaire intended to gather information on the state of the Catholic laity. As a staff member of the National Conference of Catholic Bishops of the United States at that time, I was given the job of preparing a synthesis of the replies from American dioceses. The results, submitted to the Holy See in the spring of 1986, have not been published up to now, but they make instructive reading. Here are excerpts.

> 1. *Has the teaching of the Second Vatican Council concerning the place and task of the laity in the Church and in the world been welcomed, understood, and properly presented in the local churches, with particular reference to the laity themselves? What concrete initiatives have been undertaken to achieve this goal?*

Assessments of what has been achieved since Vatican II vary, but three themes stand out.

First, the conciliar teaching has been understood and welcomed where bishops and pastors have made serious, continuing efforts to present it; where these are efforts are lacking, the teaching is not understood and appreciated.

Second, while the number of lay people actively involved in some aspect of the Church's work has increased greatly since Vatican II, they constitute a small minority among the total number of laity.

Third, lay participation is commonly understood as meaning involvement only in the programs and activities of the Church. Few lay people understand or are committed to the apostolate in the secular world.

Many laity are under the impression that Vatican II was concerned only with liturgical renewal; believing this, they believe that the Council has been fully implemented. ("After all," one respondent explained ironically, "the Mass is in English and the altar has been turned around.") They are unaware of what the Council taught about the role of the laity. . . .

Several respondents said lay people find the emphasis since the Council on individual responsibility to be confusing. One remarked that it is now common for the laity to pick and choose among Church teachings, accepting some and rejecting others.

On the positive side, there has been a significant increase in lay participation in Church ministries, structures, and programs. Liturgical renewal, parish and diocesan pastoral councils, RCIA, and a number of spiritual formation programs have contributed to this. Diocesan programs and institutions for the education and formation of lay people are helpful where they exist.

2. *Twenty years after the Council, in your particular churches, what are the positive fruits derived from the Council, and what are the new problems that the laity must face in relation to their vocation and mission?*

There has been a great increase in understanding and acceptance of the lay role among a significant minority. Many actively seek to develop their interior lives through participation in spiritual renewal programs and Bible study. These people are disposed to become active in lay ministries, parish and diocesan councils, Catholic education, etc.

Collaboration and shared responsibility between priests and laymen have increased enormously. One sign of growing maturity is the emergence of team ministries involving priests, religious, and laity.

Still, lay-clergy collaboration is spotty and even nonexistent in many places; often there are significant differences among parishes within the same diocese. Some priests feel threatened by an active laity and resist lay involvement; some laity are overly aggressive and demanding in their approaches to the clergy; these attitudes lead to tensions. Elsewhere, committed laymen are resented by their lay peers. It is common for the same handful of people to attempt to sustain virtually all parish programs; this can lead to "burnout". Low salaries are a problem for lay professionals employed by the Church. The permanent diaconate is sometimes perceived as reducing the need for lay involvement or otherwise diminishing the role of the laity.

While lay participation in ministries and Church-related activities has grown, there has been no corresponding increase in lay commitment to evangelization and the renewal of the temporal order. Nothing comparable to the Catholic Action of the 1940s and 1950s has emerged to elicit and channel lay activism, although several respondents suggested that the pro-life movement has this potential.

There is a widespread lack of education and formation for the laity. There are also serious questions about the selection and certification of lay ministers. "What we are experiencing now", one diocese said, "is much goodwill, a great deal of desire, and only shallow preparation and shallow depths of commitment."

3. *In this period and on the basis of the fullest understanding of God's plan that the whole Church be the "universal sacrament of salvation", how has the consciousness of the necessity and irreplaceability of the pastoral mission of the laity matured? Or has this maturity been based on contingent factors such as, for example, the scarcity of priests?*

Opinions differ. Some see a genuine growth in consciousness of the pastoral mission of the laity arising from their vocation and membership in the Church; others say developments have generally been triggered by the shortage of priests and religious.

One diocese, striking a middle ground, offered this comment: "There has been a remarkable expansion of lay ministry, primarily at the parish level but also at the diocesan level. This development can be traced directly to the Second Vatican Council and its emphasis on the role of the laity within the

Church. [But] this growth has also been stimulated by contingent factors, such as the expediency of recruiting lay staffs to make up for the shortage of priests and religious."

The same diocese, echoing a point made by others, added that "unfortunately, this has also hindered the full and widespread development of the conciliar teaching on the mission of the laity in the world. . . . Although there are notable exceptions, the Church does not often highlight and affirm the gifts and responsibilities of the laity to transform the social order."

To appreciate these remarks fully, not only they but the Church must be viewed in their cultural context. To a considerable extent, Western culture today is shaped and dominated by entrenched secular humanism.

In saying this, several crucial distinctions must be kept in mind. "Secular", "secularization", and "secularism" all sound very much the same, but they signify diverse realities requiring significantly different responses from religious believers.

There are good and bad aspects to secularization, understood as the process by which the autonomy of temporal values and structures is asserted. "If by the autonomy of earthly affairs", remarks Vatican II, "we mean that created things and societies themselves enjoy their own laws and values which must be gradually deciphered, put to use, and regulated by men, then it is entirely right to demand that autonomy." In contrast, "if the expression, the independence of temporal affairs, is taken to mean that created things do not depend on God, and that man can use them without any reference to their Creator, anyone who acknowledges God will see how false such a meaning is."[1]

Insofar as the secularization process does tend to foster the attitude that created things do not depend on God and can be used without reference to their Creator—in other words, the attitude of secular humanism—religious believers are not at liberty to adopt just any response. Christianity

[1] *Gaudium et Spes*, 36.

has struggled for a millennium and a half to escape the smothering embrace of caesaropapism, with all its clericalist baggage, and even now this effort is not everywhere complete. Even supposing it to be possible, the solution to the challenge posed by contemporary secular humanism does *not* lie in reestablishing a theocracy, whether the ultimate authority be vested in clerical or lay rulers.

Instead, pursuing the line laid out for it by Vatican II, the Church must recognize the legitimate autonomy of the secular order while continuing to defend the political and individual liberties of persons, including the right of religious liberty. It is the teaching of the Council, and therefore of the Church, that "the right to religious freedom has its foundation in the very dignity of the human person, as this dignity is known through the revealed Word of God and by reason itself."[2]

Still, none of this provides grounds for complacency in the face of secular humanism's cultural hegemony. It may be, as Irving Kristol says, that secular humanism today is "brain dead", intellectually moribund, but that does not make its influence less virulent; as Kristol himself remarks, "Its heart continues to pump energy into all of our institutions."[3] Neither in theory nor in the lives of individual persons can this worldview be other than radically hostile to Christianity and religion generally. It is founded on rejection of the transcendent, and at its heart, as Bonhoeffer observes, lies the belief that "in all questions of importance" people simply have no need for "the 'working hypothesis' called 'God' ".[4] But if people do not need God, then neither do they need the Church—except perhaps to provide the trappings expected on significant social occasions: church weddings, church funerals, and the like. Secularization leads not to the death of religion but to its trivialization and its expulsion as a living

---

[2] *Dignitatis Humanae*, 2.
[3] "The Future of American Jewry", *Commentary* 92, no. 2, Aug. 1991.
[4] Eberhard Bethge, ed., *Letters and Papers from Prison* (New York: Macmillan, 1967), 168.

presence from the lives of individuals and the life of the community.

In the United States, Robert Bellah argues, the problems of organized religion are further complicated by the enduring influence of the Lockean myth of the social contract and the encouragement it gives to the endemic individualism of American culture. Remarking that in a "Lockean culture" religion typically is "radically subjective and privatized", Bellah writes: "Even American Catholics have been known to say, 'As long as I'm all right with Jesus, I don't need the church.' "[5] Thus religious individualism collaborates with the secular humanist strategy of marginalizing religion.

In the nature of things, nevertheless, secular humanism is incapable of giving a satisfying account of fundamental human experiences like suffering and death, nor can it supply a solid basis, impervious to the utilitarian calculus of greater goods and lesser evils, for the defense of human rights and liberty. It points ultimately to the conclusion that life is an absurd episode in an absurd universe. Hence the irremediable sickness of secularized Western culture today; as Walter Kasper remarks, "The death of God becomes the death of man."[6]

The signs of secularization's impact upon American Catholics are impossible to ignore. Opinion polls routinely find that many people who identify themselves as Catholics reject basic elements of Catholic belief and practice. The pick-and-choose Catholicism of those who adopt elements of the Catholic Tradition that suit them while repudiating the rest is a universal phenomenon. These people make up the Catholic wing of that body of "consumer Christians" of whom Bellah says that they "shop for the best package deal they can get, and

---

[5] "Leadership Viewed from the Vantage Point of American Culture", *Origins* 20, no. 14 (Sept. 13, 1990): 220.

[6] "Nature, Grace, and Culture: On the Meaning of Secularization", in David L. Schindler, ed., *Catholicism and Secularization in America* (Huntington, Ind.: Our Sunday Visitor Books, 1990), 39.

when they find a better deal they have little hesitation about switching".[7]

There is nothing essentially new about all this. Even before the end of Vatican II, one finds a liberal lay intellectual of the day, Daniel Callahan, extolling unbounded doctrinal pluralism:

> For if the non-Catholic must be allowed to follow his conscience, then so surely must the Catholic. That means the conscience of the Catholic dissenter, even of the apostate and heretic, must be respected. . . . The fact that the Church has been slow of late in condemning doctrinal aberrations, willing to tolerate bold new lines of theological speculation, and reluctant to resort to excommunication, suggests that practice is now well ahead of theory. The result one might hope for is the minimizing of . . . situations in which the Catholic believes himself forced to choose between suppressing honest doubts about this or that article of the faith . . . and leaving the Church.[8]

As a prediction of the evolution of American Catholicism, this has proved strikingly accurate. But it is even more striking for its unconscious clericalism. Note the false dichotomy (for those who wish to remain within the Church, the alternative to assent is the suppression of doubt), and especially the legalism of Callahan's approach, so typical of the clericalist mentality: in this view, communion with the Church depends on whether or not the authorities impose ecclesiastical sanctions ("reluctant . . . to resort to excommunication") rather than on the individual's perseverance in his personal commitment of faith.

What a difference three decades make . . . or do they? Here is Anna Quindlen, op-ed columnist of the *New York Times*, explaining in 1992 how she was educated in Catholic

---

[7] Bellah, 219.

[8] "Freedom and the Layman", in John Courtney Murray, S. J., ed., *Freedom and Man* (New York: P. J. Kenedy & Sons, 1965), 164–65.

doctrine: "That was a classic way in which you learn everything about a subject and discard that which you think is nonsense"; here is Quindlen on her grounds for believing she is not a "bad Catholic": "Because I know that I represent many, many Catholics out there who feel the same way that I do"; and here is Quindlen, a prochoicer ("Isn't it possible that this is neither nonlife nor life?"), explaining her concept of "the Church" in the context of her views on abortion: "A group of unmarried men handing down dogma".[9] Less intellectually precise than Callahan three decades earlier, Quindlen is no less devoted to cafeteria-style doctrinal pluralism, legalistic thinking that settles ecclesial membership by majority vote (someone whose opinions are widely shared cannot be a "bad Catholic"), and a clericalist ecclesiology (ultimately, "the Church" is "a group of unmarried men handing down dogma", i.e., the Pope and bishops).

Different people take different views of the present condition of American Catholicism as it is exemplified in Anna Quindlen and others like her. Three distinct, widely held interpretations are common: Here is a lamentable falling-off from the doctrinal and disciplinary purity of the past, which cries out for restoration; here is a welcome and presumably permanent acceptance of radical pluralism *within* the Church as well as outside her; here is a transitional phase, marked by extreme pluralism, on the way to a new consensus in the American Church—a consensus that will be far less rigorous in matters of belief and morality than the consensus of the past.

None of these three interpretations, as we shall see, is acceptable.

Adopting one or the other of the latter two, some observers take a resolutely positive view of American Catholicism in

[9] Alexander M. Santora, interview with Anna Quindlen, *Commonweal*, Feb. 14, 1992.

its present disarray. So, for example, one sentimental journalistic account concludes with this bit of whistling in the dark: "Unlike 25 years ago, when thousands of American Catholics became dissatisfied with the speed of change, today's Catholics will stay around. They like what their Church is gradually becoming at the local level; they believe it offers hope for the future"; the author does not explain how this cheery assessment should be squared with the fact—acknowledged earlier in his overview—that the number of American Catholics who actually take the trouble to go to church is continuing to decline.[10]

The line of reasoning of such people is fairly simple. After all, sixty million or so Americans still identify themselves as Catholics, and that is an impressive quarter of the total population; although weekly Mass attendance is down from the peak levels of the 1950s and early 1960s, the rate then was atypically high, and a very large number of Catholics still go to church, at least now and then, while many even attend Mass frequently. As for those who no longer practice their religion, they should be described as "alienated" (which places the blame on the Church) rather than, as used to be the case, "lapsed" (which placed the blame on them). Even though the number of priests and nuns has declined in the last quarter-century and, given the shortage of new priestly and religious vocations, will go on declining for the foreseeable future, the laity have become much more involved in the Church than they were before Vatican II (and since the dropoff in the priesthood and religious life results from mistaken policies like mandatory celibacy, it is a good thing insofar as it speeds up the process of change).

For those who think this way, it is axiomatic that American Catholicism came of age with the election of John F. Kennedy as President. Commenting on that, and on this school of

[10] Arthur Jones, "The New World Grows Older", *The Tablet*, Jan. 25, 1992.

thought as a whole, a critic remarks, "This begs the question of whether 'coming of age' . . . involves something more than acceptability to, that is, becoming like, the larger culture."[11] For however one feels about the experience of assimilation into the larger culture, there is no doubt that American Catholics have been assimilated. So, for example, noting the precipitous numerical decline in Catholic schools since the mid-1960s (in 1965–66 there were 13,292 elementary and secondary institutions with 5.7 million students, whereas in 1989–90 the numbers were 8,792 schools and 2.58 million students, and still dropping), a review of trends in private schooling casually links what has happened to the self-evident fact that "this group [Catholics] has assimilated".[12] Although Church leadership has yet to come to grips with the implications of cultural assimilation, assimilation itself is a fact.

As this suggests, there is an unpleasant alternative to the sentimental, cheerful view. With regard to virtually everything measurable and quantifiable—except the number of those calling themselves Catholics (swollen by, among other things, a very substantial influx of Hispanic immigrants, for whom the Church is now hard pressed to provide effective pastoral programs)—the experience of the Church in the United States during the last three decades has been one of steady and accelerating institutional decline.

Now we may be entering an era of gradual institutional collapse. We have already seen some of the evidence for this. Some religious communities of women seem destined virtually to disappear. Priestless parishes and priestless Sundays are spreading as the number of clergy falls more and more sharply. Neither numerically nor in other ways is the perma-

---

[11] Glenn W. Olsen, "The Meaning of Christian Culture: A Historical View", in Schindler, 120.

[12] Bruce S. Cooper and Grace Dondero, "Survival, Change and Demands on America's Private Schools: Trends and Policies", *Educational Foundations* 5, no. 1 (Winter 1991): 51–74.

nent diaconate able to fill the gap. Even though some lay Catholics have become more active in ministries and other programs of the Church, most remain passive and indifferent. Church-sponsored institutions of all sorts are declining—for example, Catholic elementary and secondary schools. A large and growing financial crisis at all levels in the Church is forcing dioceses throughout the country to cut staff and programs. And, as far as beliefs and attitudes are concerned, vast numbers of nominal Catholics neither believe as Catholics believe nor practice what Catholics are meant to practice.

Yet the "American Church", as it has come to be called, remains wistfully committed to the notion that the Catholic community in the United States is in basically healthy condition and will be even *more* healthy once the dead hand of Roman intervention and control has finally been shaken off. Leaving aside the ecclesiology that underlies it, this is a naïve view. How healthy is the Church in a time and place where many of its nominal members do not believe what Catholics believe, do not practice what Catholics practice, and, on sensitive moral and religious questions, are more influenced by the worldview of Western secularism than the worldview of Catholic Christianity? What do Vatican interventions have to do with any of this? One thinks of words addressed to the Church of Sardis: "You have the name of being alive, and you are dead."[13]

Shortly after the close of Vatican II, the philosopher Jacques Maritain gave voice to his frustration at finding so many Catholics engaged in a peculiar exercise. He called it "kneeling before the world". Although the practice existed among both clergy and laity, he observed, "It is the clergy who set the example."[14] By "kneeling before the world" he meant

[13] Rev 3:1.   [14] Maritain, 68.

the uncritical acceptance on the part of Catholics of secular standards and values leading to the "temporalization of Christianity"—that is, to a radical devaluing of transcendent religious faith.

It is significant that Jacques Maritain, of all people, came to hold this view. An important intellectual influence on Pope Paul VI, Maritain was for decades a leading exponent of the Christian humanism that Vatican II had embraced just a few years before. His cry of alarm was not that of an integralist frozen in the rote suspicion of "the world" prevailing in some ecclesiastical circles before the Council. It was the deeply felt concern of a man who, having led the way in the effort to recapture for the Church a positive appreciation of the secular order, now had to confront the fact that, with sickening rapidity, many of his coreligionists, including many among the clerical leadership class, had swung from a blindered rejection of the secular order to an equally blindered acceptance of it.

In the years since Maritain wrote, the problem of Catholic kneeling to the world has, if anything, grown worse because it has been institutionalized and accepted as normal. At this point in the Church's age-old struggle to strike a balance between the polar heresies of Manichaeanism and Pelagianism (and among all the variants, subspecies, and mutations of the corresponding schools of thought cast up from God knows what depths of the psyche), the pendulum, at least in the secularized West, has swung leadenly toward the latter. Here, too, we can discern the dialectic of clericalism at work. Where once the old-fashioned clericalist mentality looked askance at the world and the merely human, now by way of reaction many Catholics have adopted the world's value system as their own.

Freely borrowing from popular psychology, the modern Pelagianism operates on the assumption either that there is no such thing as original sin or else that Christ's redemptive act eradicated its consequences in men. Thus a theologian whom I have cited earlier does not hesitate to affirm, "Christian faith confesses... that in *Jesus Christ God and the world are perfectly reconciled forever.*"[15] But as a matter of fact, this is *not* what Christian Faith confesses. Faith confesses that, even though the task of reconciliation has in principle been perfectly accomplished in Jesus Christ, its efficacious carrying-out in individuals depends upon human choices; salvation through the merits of Christ requires our freely willed co-operation with God. That this should be so, rather than that God impose salvation upon us willy-nilly, reflects God's respect for human freedom and responsibility and also is a necessary condition of interpersonal love (in this case, the love between men and God). As long as this great human-divine drama continues, reconciliation between God and the world, though real, nevertheless will remain incomplete and will be marked by tension.

Thus the Council of Trent teaches with admirable clarity that "even though Christ did die for all (see 2 Cor 5:15), still all do not receive the benefit of his death, but only those with whom the merit of his Passion is shared".[16] And thus, as Vatican II insists, the gospel must be preached and the means of salvation "spread abroad to the ends of the earth" precisely so that "what He once accomplished for the salvation of all may in the course of time come to achieve its effect in all".[17]

The thrust of today's Pelagianism would render this enterprise pointless. If there is no longer any alienation between mankind and God, then all are assured of salvation; and if all are assured of salvation, why bother preaching the gospel?

This is not the place for listing all the practical ramifications such attitudes have for Catholics and Catholic life, but one deserves mention: the confusion about "Catholic identity" that they foster. What does it mean to *be* Catholic in the

---

[15] Parent, 187.
[16] Decree on Justification, chap. 3.
[17] *Ad Gentes,* 3.

United States today? For the most part, Catholics of previous generations seemed to know; now it is far from clear. The liberal Catholic journal *Commonweal* offers a poignant formulation of the situation: "At last, Catholics have everything immigrant generations worked for—except an immigrant church, vigorous, disciplined, trusted."[18] More than just nostalgic pining for the past, that reflects the recognition that a significant element of the collective moral identity of American Catholics has been lost.

Many people have called attention to the consequences, applauding or deploring them according to their ideological biases. Few, however, would seriously disagree with this relatively dispassionate account by Avery Dulles:

> The tide since Vatican Council II has been running heavily toward accommodationism. Middle-aged adults constitute the last generation of Catholics raised with a strong sense of Catholic identity. Most younger Catholics look upon themselves first of all as Americans and only secondarily as Catholics. . . . Catholic schools are becoming less numerous and less distinctively Catholic. Catholic colleges and universities, while in some cases expanding, have lost much of their religious character. A certain vague religiosity perdures among the young, but it is that of "communal Catholics" not strongly committed to the doctrines and structures of their church.[19]

Clericalism is hardly the only cause of this complex crisis, but it makes a major contribution to it by separating the Church from secular culture and by introducing a parallel split—between religious commitment and worldly interests—into the lives of individual Catholics.

Thanks to the dialectic of clericalism, these attitudes remain alive and healthy today, with the balance now falling for many Catholics on the side of "worldly interests" as against

---

[18] "Re-Generating Catholicism", *Commonweal*, Jan. 27, 1990.

[19] "Catholicism and American Culture: The Uneasy Dialogue", *America*, Jan. 27, 1990.

"religious commitment". Often, too, even those with active devotional lives remain passive and apathetic toward other dimensions of religious commitment. Decent people, even exemplary in many ways, they nevertheless display little sense of vocation and apostolic responsibility. In their view—a view shaped by clericalist assumptions—these expressions of "religion" are the responsibility of priests and nuns; the role of the laity is limited to inward-looking, privatized devotions, whether these take old-fashioned preconciliar forms (novenas and the Rosary) or more modern postconciliar forms (experimental liturgies, prayer groups, etc.).

To be sure, some laymen are active in ministries and in the programs and institutions of the Church. But this very fact risks communicating a deadly message: a layman who does not feel called to engage in "ministry" or to work for the Church has no ecclesial task beyond those individualistic, minimalistic religious observances absolutely required of the laity. For these people, the famous split between faith and daily life[20] is a central element in their experience of being Catholic.

Meanwhile the clergy have problems of their own, often summed up in the expression "identity crisis". Of course, many priests know perfectly well who they are and suffer no doubts about their role, but others apparently find it hard to define their place in a Church where many functions previously reserved to clerics are now performed by laymen and the number of clergy is declining. Partly in response, it seems, clerics since Vatican II (and even before: recall the worker-priests in postwar France) have engaged in a number of experiments consciously or unconsciously intended to establish for themselves a new relationship with the secular order. These range from relatively simple, but hardly unimportant, expedients like wearing lay garb in public to holding public office or, in the case of those who are sufficiently well known to

---

[20] *Gaudium et Spes*, 43.

attract attention, making pronouncements about political and economic questions. Whatever else might be said of them, these identity experiments, as reactions against the clericalism of an earlier age, express the very same clericalist confusions over vocation, ministry, and apostolate and the forms these should take for clerics on the one hand and laymen on the other.

At this point, it will be helpful to illustrate the current state of affairs, including the working of the clericalist dialectic, in two areas that are of central importance in the lives of most laymen: marriage and work.

Christian history is marred by a certain suspicion of sexuality and marriage. Although the Church has never formally embraced such views, Christians themselves, in contending with various dualistic systems over the ages, have been influenced by what they fought against. While plainly it is "not Christian", nevertheless "this uneasiness about the fact of being male and female is part of the climate in which the Church has lived for most of its history."[21]

For this and other reasons, there has been a tendency to view marriage as a compromise solution, a kind of concession to people unwilling or unable to live as celibates. From this perspective, the choice of marriage in and of itself condemns one to an inferior condition in religious matters. This mindset "has always appeared in the guise of religion", and its proponents, "whatever name they take, are always a select few, more interested than most in the things of God. They are always the 'Pure Ones', who have the rest of the Church at a tactical disadvantage, being forced to defend what is easy."[22] As a correspondent remarks, "If one thinks of mar-

---

[21] Joseph E. Kerns, S. J., *The Theology of Marriage: The Historical Development of Christian Attitudes toward Sex and Sanctity in Marriage* (New York: Sheed and Ward, 1964), 22.
[22] Ibid.

riage too much in terms of a *remedium concupiscentiae,* if one sees the marriage act too much as a kind of 'legalized lust', justified only because of its procreative powers, then it is only natural that a religiously serious person will prefer to bypass the married state altogether."[23]

Suspicion of sex and marriage is not the whole story, however. If the Church throughout her history has had to struggle against versions of Manichaean dualism like Jansenism, while resisting the subtler tendency, encouraged by Neoplatonism, to instrumentalize bodily, temporal goods, it also has been obliged to contest repeatedly with the Pelagian mind-set and its false optimism about human nature. Today, reactions against the prudery and overemphasis on sin and guilt that are said to have been prevalent in the not so distant Catholic past have revived the ancient Pelagian attitudes among many, and these are now visible in such things as the widespread acceptance of contraception among Catholics. Adding to the witches' brew in the American context, as Robert Bellah points out, is individualism's influence upon views of sex and marriage. "Instead of the individual 'belonging' to the family," he quotes a legal scholar as saying, "it is the family which is coming to be at the service of the individual."[24]

There is a solution in the contemporary expression of Catholic doctrine on marriage, family, and sex—a body of teaching found in Vatican II, the writings of Paul VI and John Paul II, and other sources. The Council proposes a healthy vision of conjugal love: "Such love, merging the human with the divine, leads the spouses to a free and mutual gift of themselves, a gift providing itself by gentle affection and by deed. Such love pervades the whole of their lives. Indeed, by its generous activity it grows better and grows greater. Therefore it far excels mere erotic inclination, which, selfishly pursued,

---

[23] John Crosby, in a letter to the author.
[24] Bellah, 219.

soon enough fades wretchedly away."[25] But pernicious attitudes generated by the ecclesiastical and secular cultures of past and present make it difficult for many Catholics to interiorize such thinking.

With regard to work, too, one finds a similar pattern of oscillating between extremes, without settling upon a stable and productive middle ground. No doubt Catholic laymen over the centuries always have managed to find positive meaning and value in their work, but they have not always received much encouragement from those who theorized and theologized about it. The tendency instead has been to consider work a punishment for original sin and a distraction from religious duties.

There are many reasons for that. One lies in the lasting influence upon Western culture of the Greco-Roman idea that only in the cultivation of leisure is it possible to lead a genuinely human life, while work, though appropriate enough for slaves, is intrinsically unworthy of anyone who aspires to the higher things.

The problem also is closely linked to the clericalist-monastic mentality and its devaluing of secular activities. As a consequence of the monastic ideal's influence on spiritual theology, "ecclesiastical tasks came to be considered as the only really sanctifying ones. This in effect closed the way to recognition of the sanctifying value of everyday work."[26] The results have been predictable: "Until quite recently, spiritual theology knew nothing, said nothing, about the subject of work."[27] Of three well-known manuals of spiritual theology in the first half of the twentieth century (Tanqueray, Garrigou-Lagrange, and de Guibert), only one discusses the sanctification of work—and it devotes only three pages to the subject. It

---

[25] *Gaudium et Spes*, 49.
[26] José Luís Illanes, *On the Theology of Work* (Dublin, Ireland: Four Courts Press, 1982), 26.
[27] Ibid.

is as if what most people spend most of their time doing were irrelevant to the interior life.

But if, where work was concerned, the characteristic error of the past, distant and not so distant, was excessive otherworldliness, the characteristic error of the present is a kind of mirror image, both different and surprisingly alike. It is the tendency to treat work as a free-fire zone where people do whatever they must to get ahead and achieve individualistic fulfillment.

The results are rich in irony. Unhealthy contemporary attitudes toward work find their pathological flowering in "workaholism"; persons so afflicted attach inordinate significance to their work—to the point that other forms of activity, other ways of participating in human goods, are sacrificed to the all-encompassing job. But workaholics take work too seriously precisely because they do not know how to take it seriously enough. Not only do they plunge into work to the exclusion of other human goods that should *not* be excluded; they also behave this way because, at bottom, they cannot imagine that God really cares *what* they do on the job. Work is something separate and apart from that area in their lives designated "God", "transcendence", or simply "ultimate meaning and value". Although they are obsessed with work, work has as little real value for them as it has for those who hold distorted notions about leisure or asceticism.

As with marriage, family, and sex, there is a more balanced view of work in the recent teaching of the Church as well as in the spirituality encouraged by various lay groups and movements. This view revolves around the themes of co-creation and co-redemption, as these are found in Vatican II (*Gaudium et Spes*) and in the writing of John Paul II (e.g., *Laborem Exercens*).

Considered as co-creation, work is among the most important means available to man for cooperating with God in realizing the as yet unrealized elements of his plan for creation. "Hence it is clear", the Council remarks, "that men are not deterred by the Christian message from building up the world, or impelled to neglect the welfare of their fellows. They are, rather, more stringently bound to do these very things."[28]

As for co-redemption, work's painful aspects express the fact that, like other disagreeable things in life arising either from sin or from the human condition scarred by sin, work-related suffering has a redemptive value in association with the redemptive activity of Christ, including especially his human suffering. In his apostolic letter "On the Christian Meaning of Human Suffering", Pope John Paul cites Saint Paul's words in Colossians to make this point: "Now I rejoice in my sufferings for your sake, and in my flesh I complete what is lacking in Christ's afflictions for the sake of his body, that is, the Church" (Col 1:24).[29]

Still more fundamentally, as we shall see at greater length below, the definitive meaning and value of all human activity, including work, are clarified in Vatican II's teaching linking our striving to realize human goods in this life and our perfect fulfillment in those same goods in heaven.[30] Thus, as with other problems arising from clericalist attitudes, the elements of a Christian solution to the problem of work are now in place; but—as also is true of many another problem in the lives of today's Catholics—clericalism and its progeny make it harder to see and implement the solution.

Clericalism also creates grave difficulties *within* the Church. The clericalist mind-set contributes in many ways to the confusion and bitterness that often color discussions of ecclesial relationships today. Here, as often as not, the operative idea is power.

Yet from a certain perspective power is not even an appropriate issue in defining relationships within the community

---

[28] *Gaudium et Spes*, 34.
[29] *Salvifici Doloris*, 24.
[30] See *Gaudium et Spes*, 38, 39.

of Faith. That is especially so when power has its ordinary meaning: the capacity not only to do as one pleases but also to impose one's will on others in order to compel them to do as pleases one. That is not how brothers and sisters in Jesus Christ might be expected to relate to one another.

Even when power has a more positive meaning—a capacity for serving and helping others—the temptation remains strong, human nature being what it is, to revert unconsciously to power's less elevated meaning and once more begin treating ecclesial relationships as structures of domination. Partly in reaction, it is common in Catholic circles today for people to emphasize the distinction between power and authority: power then signifies coercing others, while authority means inviting their free response to proposals aimed at fostering the common good; and naturally it is authority, not power, that supplies the preferred model for understanding governance and jurisdiction in the Church.

Governance and jurisdiction are indispensable in ecclesial life. No human society can exist without some form of authority for decision making (minimally, as an instrument to facilitate a process in which the other members of the society also participate) and to organize joint actions that carry out decisions made in pursuit of the society's common purposes. It is no different in the Church. Both by the requirements of any society and by the specific will of Christ, this communion of men enjoying radical equality and dignity is also, according to the testimony of the New Testament, hierarchically structured. As Paul's image of the Church as the body of Christ makes clear, there is a necessary, divinely willed subordination of some members to others for purposes of decision making and the directing of common activity.

Especially since the Council, however, strenuous efforts have been made to expunge the understanding of ecclesial authority as a form of power conceived in terms of domination and submission; in its place, the idea of ecclesial authority as a mode of service has repeatedly been emphasized. In this view, the supreme exemplar of authority that serves is Jesus, who "came not to be served but to serve".[31]

For example, the Council says of bishops that in exercising "authority and sacred power" within the particular churches that they govern, they act "only for the edification of their flock in truth and holiness, remembering that he who is greater should become as the lesser and he who is the more distinguished, as the servant (cf. Lk 22:26–27)".[32] Similarly, priests, "prudent cooperators with the episcopal order as well as its aids and instruments, are called to serve the People of God".[33] Several years later Pope Paul VI addressed the question of whether this means the Church now is to be "governed by the faithful, to the service of whom the bishops are bound". His answer of course was no, for "the bishops are constituted by the Holy Spirit to shepherd the Church of God": "To shepherd, *poimainein*—this is the decisive word, a word that with the depth of its meaning links in a marvelous way the juridical charism of authority with the sovereign charism of love. It gives the pastor his true Gospel figure, that of goodness . . . and that of the disciple of Christ, set up to exercise the 'care of souls' which demands a complete gift of self, an inexhaustible spirit of sacrifice."[34]

But if all that is so, someone might ask, what really is the problem? Considering all the statements of policy and principle since Vatican II affirming that hierarchical *authority* is essentially a mode of *pastoral service* in love, has not at least this aspect of the problem of clericalism been settled? Surely the day of monarchical bishops and baronial pastors is over. Do not priests, as the Council urged, now "deal with other men as with brothers"?[35]

---

[31] Mt 20:28.
[32] *Lumen Gentium*, 27.
[33] Ibid., 28.
[34] Homily on the Meaning of Ecclesial Power, Sept. 22, 1974.
[35] *Presbyterorum Ordinis*, 3.

Despite pockets of resistance here and there, these beautiful ideals do indeed appear much closer to being realized, at least in the Church in the United States, than they have been for many centuries. If the problem of clericalism were simply a matter of *style* in interpersonal relations, we would be entitled not only to hail the progress since Vatican II but also to look forward to clericalism's total demise in the foreseeable future. Unfortunately, the problem is not that simple. Much more than style is at issue.

Consider a basic question: From where, after all, does clerical authority ultimately come? In fact, there are conflicting theories.

Before the Council, it was commonly held that, while the sacramental power of the priesthood comes from orders, power in the sense of *jurisdiction* comes from God to the Pope, from the Pope to the bishops, and from the bishops to the priests. In this pyramidal model, not only is the Pope the Vicar of Christ—the bishop is the vicar of the Pope, and the priest, one might say, is the bishop's vicar. The laity, of course, lie at the very bottom of the pyramid and lack any power at all.

The situation is summed up in the schema on the Church prepared for, but not voted on by, Vatican Council I. It observes that the Church is "not a society of equals . . . not only because some of the faithful are clerics and some laymen, but especially because in the Church there is a power of divine institution, by which some are authorized to sanctify, teach, and govern, and others do not have this authority".[36] Of this understanding of the Church Avery Dulles remarks that it "views the clergy, especially the higher clergy, as the source of all power and initiative . . . the faithful people play a passive role".[37]

Recognizing the drawbacks of such a theory, a more recent

---

[36] In Clarkson et al., 93.   [37] *Models of the Church*, 43.

account has it that both the bishop and the rest of the clergy receive their jurisdictional authority directly from the sacrament of orders (the nonepiscopal clergy to a lesser degree than the bishops, of course). This way of thinking is reflected, for example, in Vatican II's affirmation that bishops "govern the particular churches entrusted to them as the vicars and ambassadors of Christ . . . nor are they to be regarded as vicars of the Roman Pontiff, for they exercise an authority which is proper to them";[38] while priests, as "cooperators with the episcopal order", are called to "sanctify and govern under the bishop's authority that part of the Lord's flock entrusted to them".[39] Union with the Pope is essential in the case of bishops, and union with the bishop is essential in the case of priests; but bishops are not merely representatives of the Pope, nor are priests merely the bishop's representatives.

This is all very well for bishops and even, up to a point, for priests. But what about the laity? Vatican II's teaching sheds light on relationships within the clerical hierarchy, but the theory underlying it makes no provision for laymen. If power in the Church (or authority or whatever other name one wishes to give the reality involved) comes only from the sacrament of orders, then of course the laity have no proper claim to it and can only share in it (if at all) by the sufferance of the clergy.

Even if, as is now the case, the clergy generally seem to take a generous and forthcoming approach to the matter, still, from the point of view of laymen, this state of affairs is no essential improvement upon the pyramidal ecclesiology before Vatican II. Indeed, some even contend that the new thinking embraced by the Council and embodied in the 1983 Code of Canon Law provides "impetus . . . for the emergence of a Church more clerical than ever before in its history".[40]

[38] *Lumen Gentium*, 27.
[39] Ibid., 28.
[40] Ladislas Orsy, "Priests and People", *The Tablet*, June 9, 1990.

This probably overstates the case. After all, the structures of the Church and the attitudes prevalent among Catholics have been *exceedingly* clericalist for a very long time; now at least countervailing forces are at work to overcome clericalism and its debilitating effects. But even so, such dour prognoses do call attention to the present curiously mixed state of affairs in the Church as she really is: we are a sharply divided community in which old and new forms of clericalism coexist with yearnings for a nonclericalist ecclesial life that has yet to find either its generally accepted theoretical grounding or its universally recognized practical expression.

Historically, as we have seen, one way of giving at least some power to laymen has been to say it comes to them by delegation or concession, as a participation in clerical power. Today this attitude frequently is the moving force behind benevolent experiments in clerical power-sharing usually designated "lay ministries". The problems this raises are obvious: the approach implies, or can easily be interpreted as implying, that laymen can have an active part in the Church's mission only by sharing in power that properly belongs to clerics and that the fullest expression of their identity as *christifideles* lies in doing, more or less, what priests do.

Just as, generally speaking, this was the thrust of Catholic Action's model of lay apostolate, so lay ministries and other contemporary power-sharing arrangements in the Church tend to continue into the present day certain of the undesirable attitudes and assumptions of Catholic Action.

In saying this, it is necessary to repeat what was said earlier: in its day, Catholic Action was an important step forward in winning recognition, among the laity as well as among priests, that laymen do have important work to do in carrying on the mission of the Church. Considering the many centuries during which religious passivity was considered the normal condition of the Catholic laity, this was important progress.

But this progress was limited, for, as we have seen, it

rested on the assumption that the lay activity involved in Catholic Action was a supplement to and extension of hierarchical ministry; thus explanations of Catholic Action never tired of declaring it to be the participation of the laity in the apostolate of the hierarchy. As such, any form of activity or structure aspiring to the name Catholic Action required a hierarchical mandate and, to one degree or another, hierarchical control.[41] This is understandable—just as now it is understandable that lay ministers, properly so called, should receive some kind of formal commissioning or "institution" at the hands of representatives of the clerical hierarchy. Such ceremonies emphasize that lay ministers do not engage in ministry on their own initiative or at the mandate of the community at large but only by way of participation in the work of the hierarchy, whose approval they must have.

But this leaves a fundamental question: Does participation in the apostolates (or ministries) of clerics exhaust lay participation in the mission of the Church? As far as the laity's ecclesial role goes—is that all? The clericalist mentality tends to suppose it is. Plainly it is not.

Because they have been baptized and confirmed, Catholic laymen have an intrinsic obligation and a corresponding right to participate in the work of the Church. The obligation and right do not come by clerical concession or delegation any more than they are conferred by community mandate. They belong to laymen simply inasmuch as they are *christifideles,* members of the community of Faith.

Vatican II makes these points very clearly in a number of places. In a key passage near the beginning of Chapter Four (on the laity) of the Dogmatic Constitution on the Church, the Council teaches that laymen "are by baptism made one body with Christ and are established among the People of God. They are in their own way made sharers in the priestly, prophetic, and kingly functions of Christ. They carry out

---

[41] Ferree, 27.

their own part in the mission of the whole Christian people with respect to the Church and the world."[42] This is a quantum leap beyond the clericalist assumptions permeating Catholic Action as well as beyond the view of lay ministries held today by many priests and laity.

But not only does the ecclesial role of the laity include participating by intrinsic obligation and right in the mission of the Church; the teaching of Vatican II makes it clear that it is proper to this *ecclesial* role that laymen should be immersed in *secular* affairs—in "the world"—and should there carry on an apostolate that is properly theirs. Their secular quality, Pope John Paul emphasizes, is not just a sociological datum pertaining to the laity but also a central part of their theological identity: "Thus for the lay faithful, to be present and active in the world is not only an anthropological and sociological reality, but in a specific way, a theological and ecclesiological reality as well. In fact, in their situation in the world, God manifests his plan and communicates to them their particular vocation."[43]

Of course, where clericalism's distorted view of the world and of secular interests persists (or where, for that matter, the dialectic has caused Maritain's "kneeling to the world" to take its place among clerics and laity), it will seem meaningless to say that the *ecclesial* role proper to laymen requires their involvement in the affairs of the world. Rather, "the position of the layman in the world . . . begins to be regarded as due to a lack of any vocation to a higher state, and ceases to be considered as a mission entrusted to him by Christ himself."[44]

As for laymen who wish to be religiously active, they are likely to find themselves propelled willy-nilly into a scramble for ecclesiastical power centering on Church structures and offices. But since ecclesiastical politics generally hold little charm or interest for the laity, this tends to reinforce the

[42] *Lumen Gentium*, 31.
[43] *Christifideles Laici*, 14.
[44] Del Portillo, 18.

apathy of the many even while it inflames the ambition, along with the sense of exclusion, of the few.

The practical solution to questions of power in the Church lies in a correct understanding of vocation. And the key to a correct understanding of vocation, especially as it applies to the laity, lies in a proper appreciation of baptism, confirmation, and the Eucharist. Only in reflecting upon these sacraments do we begin to comprehend what it means to say that all members of the Church are called personally by God to participate in the Church's mission. Even then a great deal of undergrowth, both historical and contemporary, must be cleared away before we can see clearly what this means.

Pope John Paul leaves no doubt about the fundamental fact: "The participation of the lay faithful in the threefold mission of Christ as Priest, Prophet and King finds its source in the anointing of Baptism, its further development in Confirmation and its realization and dynamic sustenance in the Holy Eucharist."[45] We are a long way here from the notion that lay apostolate is a participation in the apostolate of the hierarchy requiring an episcopal mandate. The vision is that expressed succinctly in Canon 211 of the 1983 Code of Canon Law: "All Christ's faithful have the obligation and the right to strive so that the divine message of salvation may more and more reach all people of all times and all places." In such statements one sees the Church attempting to unpack the meaning of a key scriptural formula: "You are a chosen race, a royal priesthood, a holy nation."[46] Here, as the Pope says, one confronts "a new aspect to the grace and dignity coming from Baptism".[47]

Old-fashioned clerical elitism is an obstacle to grasping all this and acting upon it. Bismarck, no friend of the Church, provided a stingingly perceptive description of what has, his-

---

[45] *Christifideles Laici*, 14.
[46] 1 Pet 2:9.
[47] *Christifideles Laici*, 14.

torically, been the common state of affairs among Catholics on the one hand and Protestants on the other:

> The two churches . . . have very different bases. The whole being of the Catholic Church is in her clergy, she exists and fulfills herself through them; she could go on without a community, Mass can be celebrated without a congregation; the community is useful for the affirmation of the Christian function of the Catholic Church, but it is not at all necessary for the existence of that Church. In the Protestant Church on the contrary the community is the entire foundation of the whole church: worship is unthinkable without it, the whole Protestant Church constitution rests on the community.[48]

On the Catholic side, Germain Grisez suggests, the mistake arises first of all from a misunderstanding of the principle of *in persona Christi* (in the person of Christ—as Christ's proxy, we might say) as a description of the essential role of the ordained ministry: in effect, the proxy is confused with the principal, the priest with Christ himself, with all the practical consequences that implies.

> Priests have a special service of acting *in persona Christi*, but their action is only to proxy, so that the communion is built up. And the faithful who benefit from their service also must be active, because what priests serve is a cooperative relationship, not the delivery of goods to passive recipients. [But] the false idea of mediation is a point of departure for other things: the priests become rulers, running people's lives, rather than teachers of moral truth, helping them to see what is there. . . . The priests run the Church without paying much attention to the laity—they are just matter on which to exercise "pastoral" skills. (The image of the shepherd is overworked, because it fits the clericalist idea that the faithful are dumb sheep, not members of an interpersonal relationship.) Priests lose sight of their role of service acting *in persona Christi* but take on some of Christ's majesty as if it were their own.

---

[48] Quoted in Congar, 51.

> There is an essential difference between the Christian life of priests and laity, since producer and product do not share in a common life. . . . From this follow elitism and all the rest. For a layperson to become serious about being a member of the Church and holy therefore demands that the layperson participate in properly clerical activities—get ordained, engage in a ministry, and so on. At the same time, the whole of a layperson's life in which he or she is properly active lies outside the Church; it is entirely unreligious, merely secular.[49]

The mind-set of clerical elitism naturally supposes that the Church's mission is the responsibility of the clergy. If laymen share in it at all, that is by way of clerical concession and delegation. First and foremost, though, the task of the laity is to be passive recipients of what the clergy have to give them—including directives; they are consigned to a condition of permanent dependency, with no room for the exercise of a priestly role arising from baptism or for active involvement in the Church's mission arising from intrinsic obligations and rights.

But neocongregationalism is not the answer. It throws up obstacles of its own, less obvious perhaps but no less real, to a proper understanding of the role of the laity, for it is grounded in an exaggerated view of the baptismal priesthood that confuses and hampers laymen in their efforts to exercise the true priestly role that belongs to them. This is not just a distraction from what should be the genuine concerns of clerics and laity alike; one also finds here the ultimate source of confusion regarding the question of power: finally, there *is* no question, since everyone has the same power.

Not satisfied with the fact that baptism empowers the *christifideles* to participate in the celebration of the Eucharist as the nonbaptized simply cannot do,[50] a congregationalist ecclesiology supposes that the nonordained can celebrate the Eu-

---

[49] Letter to the author.
[50] *Lumen Gentium*, 11; cf. Pope Pius XII, *Mediator Dei*.

charist. In doing so, of course, it is reacting against the clericalist assumption, common in the past, that the laity are passive spectators of the liturgy, in which priests play the only active role.

As we have seen, congregationalist and neocongregationalist thinking clashes with definitive Catholic teaching: that orders is a sacrament and that there is an essential difference between the ordained priesthood and the baptismal priesthood (Trent and Vatican II). Moreover, in collapsing the distinction between baptismal priesthood and ordained priesthood, this school of thought unwittingly undermines the baptismal priesthood whose claims it means to advance. The implication is that, in order to enjoy true ecclesial dignity and status, the nonordained must be priests just as much, and in *just the same way,* as are the ordained.

Much harm results to laymen and to priests alike. For the latter, the crisis of priestly identity is deepened and intensified. As for the laity, the climate of opinion within the Church to which this kind of thinking gives rise tends to divert their energies from the critically important apostolate that is proper to them—the apostolate in and to the secular order—while channeling them into ecclesiastical structures and offices. However positive, and even necessary, a development lay ministries may be in their place, they are *not*—as I have said before and shall say again—the form of ecclesial activity that is proper to laymen. To put it bluntly, the Catholic laity have more important things to do than "ministry".

Finally, collapsing the distinction between ordained and nonordained priesthood has the paradoxical result of reinforcing the clericalist assumption that clerics are superior. For if all members of the community are priests in essentially the same way, then those who actually *function* as ordained priests now do, preeminently in the setting of the eucharistic liturgy, must be superior to those who do not: members of the community who *in fact* do what all *in principle* could do surely must be members in a fuller sense than the rest.

For most Catholic laymen, the really serious practical question centers upon the issue of vocation.

Most, after all, are unaware of the neocongregationalist suggestion that they can offer Mass and would not be very interested in the notion if they were aware. Indeed, most probably would consider the idea outlandish—a reaction expressing the *sensus fidelium* at work in a manner to which neocongregationalists are not, understandably, anxious to call attention.

But whether they are aware of it or not, *all* Catholic laymen suffer injury from the confused and erroneous ideas about vocation that are central to the clericalist mind-set. To a great extent, clericalism and its offspring *are* the vocations crisis in the Church today. For a solution, we must turn next to the question of vocation and vocations: What is a vocation, and who really has one?

V

FROM POWER TO VOCATION

Sooner or later, anyone examining the roots of clericalism is bound to confront a fundamental question focused upon one of the basic assumptions sustaining the clericalist mind-set. Do the clerical vocation and the clerical life-style supply the standard against which to measure the vocations and life-styles of all other members of the Church?

These days, if the question is put that bluntly, not many people have trouble coming up with the "correct" answer. This is *not* what God has in mind for everyone. The clerical vocation and life-style are the standard, the norm, for those called to them, but they are not normative for the rest of us. For those *christifideles* called to be laymen, it is precisely as laity that they are meant to participate in the threefold ministry of Christ as Prophet, Priest, and King and in the mission of the Church.

But even when the clericalist mentality pays lip service to this ideal, it does not seem to grasp it very well. Old attitudes persist not far below the surface. Laymen? They have jobs, marriages, commitments, and relationships of various kinds, and no doubt some of these are important in their own way. They may even have ecclesial roles—participation in ministries that more or less resemble the work of clerics. But the laity do not, and cannot, have real vocations, since "vocation" by definition signifies the special calling of those whom God wants to be priests.

The Catholic Church teaches that laymen do have vocations. The Second Vatican Council in many places speaks of the laity and their way of life in vocational terms. Laymen, it says, "by Baptism are incorporated into Christ, are placed in the People of God, and in their own way share the priestly, prophetic and kingly office of Christ. . . . [T]he laity, by their very vocation, seek the kingdom of God by engaging in temporal affairs and by ordering them according to the plan of God."[1]

The laity have a calling that is proper to them; it is the vocation to *be* laity "and to the best of their ability to carry on the mission of the whole Christian people in the Church and in the world".[2] In fact, "they are mistaken who, knowing that we have here no abiding city but seek one which is to come, think that they may therefore shirk their earthly responsibilities. For they are forgetting that by the faith itself they are more than ever obliged to measure up to these duties, each according to his proper vocation."[3]

Pope John Paul II repeats and expands on the Council's teaching. In *Christifideles Laici* he writes, "The participation of the lay faithful in the threefold mission of Christ . . . finds its source in the anointing of baptism, its further development in confirmation, and its realization and dynamic sustenance in the Holy Eucharist."[4] He also stresses the reality of *unique, individual* vocation: "It is a participation given to each member of the lay faithful individually, inasmuch as each is one of the many who form the one body of the Lord."[5] And again:

> Being "members" of the Church takes nothing away from the fact that each Christian as an individual is "unique and unrepeatable". On the contrary, this belonging guarantees and fosters the profound sense of that uniqueness and unrepeat-

---

[1] *Lumen Gentium*, 31.
[2] Ibid.
[3] *Gaudium et Spes*, 43.
[4] *Christifideles Laici*, 15.
[5] Ibid.

ability, insofar as these very qualities are the source of variety and richness for the whole Church. Therefore, God calls the individual in Jesus Christ, each one personally by name. In this sense, the Lord's words "You go into my vineyard too", directed to the Church as a whole, come specially addressed to each member individually.[6]

If it does nothing else, this quoting of official documents at least makes clear a critically important point. The idea that laymen have vocations is not a hobbyhorse for malcontents. It is the position of the Catholic Church, and it is capable of revolutionizing the Church and changing the lives of all her members for the better.

In recent decades an understanding of vocation vastly different from the version assumed by the mentality of clericalism has been taking shape in the Church. It is crucial to solving the problem of clericalism, the vocations crisis, the separation of Faith from life, and many other ills afflicting Catholics and their Church.

According to this view, vocation has three related but distinct senses: (1) the common Christian vocation arising from baptism; (2) vocation as "state in life" or, as one of my correspondents suggests, "vocation to special service"; and (3) unique individual vocation.

For a fuller understanding of each of these meanings of vocation, let us turn to *Lumen Gentium*.

1. *The common Christian vocation.* Baptism brings about incorporation into Christ and, as a result, membership in "that messianic people [which] has for its head Christ"—the people of God, the New Covenant community, the Church.[7] In this sense, Hans Urs von Balthasar remarks, Christians "belong to one common state": the state of the baptized *christifideles*.[8]

---

[6] Ibid., 28.
[7] *Lumen Gentium,* 9.
[8] *The Christian State of Life* (San Francisco: Ignatius Press, 1983), 142ff.

Indicating the vocation of this people, and therefore the common vocation of its individual members, in very general terms, the Council says: "Its goal is the kingdom of God, which has been begun by God Himself on earth, and which is to be further extended until it is brought to perfection by Him at the end of time. . . . Established by Christ as a fellowship of life, charity, and truth, [this people] is also used by Him as an intrument for the redemption of all, and is sent forth into the whole world as the light of the world and the salt of the earth (cf. Mt 5:13–16)."[9] Apostolate, participation in the redemptive mission of Jesus, is at the heart of the mission of the Church and the vocations of her individual members.

2. *Vocation as state in life (or vocation to special service).* In some ways, as we shall see, this is the most obscure and controversial meaning of vocation; despite (or perhaps because of) the existence of an enormous quantity of theological literature on the subject, there is need for much theological clarification regarding "states". Still, it is clear that, both in the mind of Vatican II and in actual fact, there truly are state in life vocations or vocations to special service that mediate between the common baptismal vocation shared by all and the unique individual vocation of each member of the Church.

In an important passage, the Council teaches concerning the vocations to the clerical, religious, and lay states respectively: "[B]y reason of their particular vocation [clerics] are chiefly and professedly ordained to the sacred ministry. Similarly, by their state in life, religious give splendid and striking testimony that the world cannot be transfigured and offered to God without the spirit of the beatitudes. But the laity, by their very vocation, seek the kingdom of God by engaging in temporal affairs and by ordering them according to the plan of God."[10] Whatever else might be said of the various states in life, this makes it clear that each *is* a framework for service of a particular kind.

---

[9] *Lumen Gentium*, 9.   [10] Ibid., 31.

3. *Unique individual vocation.* Vatican II speaks of individual vocation in a number of places—for example, "Fortified by so many and such powerful means of salvation, all the faithful, whatever their condition or state, are called by the Lord, *each in his own way,* to that perfect holiness whereby the Father Himself is perfect."[11] Or again, in a passage on religious: "[T]he counsels, voluntarily undertaken according to *each one's personal vocation,* contribute greatly to purification of heart and spiritual liberty."[12]

What is a unique individual vocation? In abstract terms, it is the particular calling that each member of the Church receives from God to live out the common baptismal vocation, within the framework of a particular state in life or mode of service, in this way seeking personal sanctification and also making a unique, unrepeatable contribution to the mission of the Church as a whole—the mission that essentially is the extension throughout all times and places of the redemptive work of Jesus Christ.

A renewed appreciation for the reality of individual vocation is one of the authentic gifts of the Spirit to the Church in our times. Henceforth, "when people want to speak of how one vocation is different from another . . . the distinction can never be sought in whether one person is called to the fullness of holiness or not, nor in whether a person shares in the mission of the Church or not. The distinction rests in the particular vocation each person has received."[13]

In the light of this overview, let us take a closer look at the idea of vocation as it has been developed not only by Vatican II but also in subsequent theological reflection and magisterial teaching.

First of all, it is important to be aware of the dynamic nature of vocation in all its senses. God does not summon

[11] Ibid., 11; emphasis added.
[12] Ibid., 46; emphasis added.
[13] Stephen G. Gibson, *'Called by the Lord': The Theme of Vocation in Lumen Gentium* (Rome: Pontifical University of St. Thomas Aquinas, 1990), 204.

people to passivity; he calls them to diverse forms of cooperation with Jesus in the continuation of his redemptive mission. Christian life involves a continuing unfolding of God's will and a continuing process of discernment and response on the part of Christians.

In general terms, nevertheless, certain fundamental patterns are at work in Christian life. The Council underscores this by pointing out that Christians are called to participate in Christ's triple mission.

So, according to Vatican II, the baptized are "consecrated into a spiritual house and a holy priesthood";[14] they become a "priestly community".[15] Their priesthood finds its supreme exercise in their participation in the Mass. To be sure, all do not participate in the same way, but rather "each in that way which is appropriate to himself"; still, there is a fundamental likeness marking the participation of all: "Taking part in the Eucharistic Sacrifice, which is the fount and apex of the whole Christian life, they offer the divine Victim to God, and offer themselves along with It."[16]

The baptized also express their priestly character by participation in the rest of the Church's sacramental life and worship. The Council specifically applies this to Christian wives and husbands: "[I]n virtue of the sacrament of matrimony, [they] signify and partake of the mystery of that unity and fruitful love which exists between Christ and His Church (cf. Eph 5:32). The spouses thereby help each other to attain to holiness in their married life and by the rearing and education of their children."[17]

As for participation in Jesus' prophetic office, the Council affirms that this essentially is a matter of proclaiming the gospel in deed and in word. The community of the *christifideles* "spreads abroad a living witness to [Christ], especially by means of a life of faith and charity and by offering to God

---

[14] *Lumen Gentium*, 14.
[15] Ibid., 11.
[16] Ibid.
[17] Ibid.

a sacrifice of praise, the tribute of lips which give honor to His name (cf. Heb 13:15)".[18]

In this context—participation by the community of the faithful in the prophetic mission—Vatican II reasserts the infallibility of the Church's belief "when, 'from the bishops down to the last member of the laity', it shows universal agreement in matters of faith and morals".[19] It then goes on to point out that the Spirit distributes charismatic graces "among the faithful of every rank", thereby making them "fit and ready to undertake the various tasks and offices advantageous for the renewal and upbuilding of the Church"; nevertheless, such gifts "are not to be rashly sought after", and judgment regarding their authenticity and proper use belongs to those whose own charism is expressed in holding offices of ecclesial authority.[20]

Finally, in this section of *Lumen Gentium* Vatican II speaks of the participation of the baptized in Christ's kingly mission. This, it suggests, has mainly to do with their membership in the kingdom of God, which in itself confers upon them both an evangelizing role and a responsibility for the well-being of the whole Church: "[A]mong all the nations of earth there is but one People of God, which takes its citizens from every race, making them citizens of a kingdom which is of a heavenly and not an earthly nature. . . . [T]he Catholic Church strives energetically and constantly to bring all humanity with all its riches back to Christ its Head in the unity of His Spirit. In virtue of this catholicity each individual part of the Church contributes through its special gifts to the good of the other parts and of the whole Church."[21] Perhaps one might add that the specific function of the *christifideles* under this heading lies in *ordering* according to God's plan whatever in the world it falls within their power to order.

[18] Ibid., 12.
[19] Ibid., 19.
[20] Ibid.
[21] Ibid., 13.

Here, too, we find an explanation for the hierarchical structure and diversity of roles and functions existing alongside the fundamental unity of the Church's members and their equality in dignity: "Not only, then, is the People of God made up of different peoples but even in its inner structure it is composed of various ranks. This diversity among its members arises either by reason of their duties, as is the case with those who exercise the sacred ministry for the good of their brethren, or by reason of their situation and way of life, as is the case with those many who enter the religious state and, tending toward holiness by a narrower path, stimulate their brethren by their example."[22]

So much—for now at least—for the common Christian vocation shared by all the baptized faithful, clerics, religious, and laity alike, as well as for its dynamic character as a participation in the threefold ministry of Jesus. What of vocation understood as a calling to a state in life (or a special mode of Christian service)?

As suggested, this valid meaning of vocation may also be its most obscure and controverted. The literature is a dense theological thicket involving many complex and unresolved questions about the "states" and how they are related. Whatever else might be said of it, the discussion of these matters does not appear up to now to have been of any significant benefit to the cause of the laity and their active participation in the mission of the Church.

The case of Hans Urs von Balthasar is instructive. This major Catholic theologian has been more interested in and sympathetic to the laity than most of his colleagues. Nevertheless, in *The Christian State of Life,* a dense and erudite study, von Balthasar unhesitatingly asserts the qualitative superiority of the "state of election" to the state of laymen in the world;

[22] Ibid.

and although he acknowledges that laymen *can* enter into this state of election by making a specific commitment to the evangelical counsels—for example, becoming members of secular institutes—in general, it seems, this is the state of religious and clerics. Similarly, on the far more important question of sanctity and who can achieve it, von Balthasar, while granting that holiness and heroic virtue are "attainable" in marriage, nevertheless holds their actual attainment by married persons to be "only by way of exception".[23]

Even when it comes to apostolate in and to the secular order (an area where one might reasonably expect the laity to be granted primacy), von Balthasar, despite the teaching of Vatican Council II, is reluctant to concede anything to laymen but instead manifests ambivalence. On the one hand, it "would be one-sided to claim that [the] permeation of the world is exclusively, or even primarily, the task of the laity in the world";[24] on the other hand, "it would be dilettantism today for religious and priests to believe themselves capable of solving concrete economic and sociological questions instead of expending their efforts to open the eyes of hearts of capable lay persons and encouraging them to lay the foundations of a Christian social order."[25] That is hardly a wholehearted endorsement of the idea that laymen have an important role, properly theirs, in the mission of the Church.

It goes without saying that von Balthasar is neither obtuse nor biased against the laity. But if the treatment of "states" in the thinking of this distinguished theologian is in some respects prejudicial to the laity (and so, to that extent, to

---

[23] Von Balthasar, 377–78.

[24] In light of Vatican II, von Balthasar is on safe ground in denying that the apostolate belongs "exclusively" to the laity, but he is on very weak—in fact, untenable—ground in saying it does not belong "primarily" to them: see, e.g., *Lumen Gentium*, 31.

[25] Von Balthasar, 356–57.

the real interests of the Church), one can easily imagine how matters stand in the thought of less distinguished thinkers. It is scarcely surprising that, historically, the laity have been either ignored or downgraded in discussions of vocation and states of life.

Lately a great deal of effort has gone into correcting this situation, so harmful to the Church and all her members. For, at least in practical terms, it seems somewhat beside the point whether one state of life, *precisely as a state,* enjoys superiority to another. Here—in practical terms—unique individual vocation is what counts. Each person must discern, accept, and live out that state of life and all the other circumstances of life to which God calls him.

The idea of individual vocation is not new. For example, Newman, in one of his Anglican sermons, suggests an important aspect of the reality, namely, its ongoing, contemporaneous, altogether *present* character: "For in truth we are not called once only but many times; all through our life Christ is calling us. He called us first in Baptism; but afterwards also; whether we obey His voice or not, He graciously calls us still. . . . It were well if we understood this; but we are slow to master the great truth, that Christ is, as it were, walking among us, and by His hand, or eye, or voice, bidding us follow Him. . . . The accidents and events of life are, as is obvious, one special way in which the calls I speak of come to us."[26]

Even earlier, Jean-Pierre de Caussade, writing of what he calls the "sacrament of the present moment", points to the dynamic immediacy of God's will and the Christian's response to it: "Who among us is the holiest? To try to find out is pointless. Everyone must follow the appointed path. Holiness consists in obeying God and working with him to

---

[26] "Divine Calls", in *Parochial and Plain Sermons* (San Francisco: Ignatius Press, 1987), 1569–70.

the best of our abilities. Making comparisons between various states is meaningless, for holiness is not to be looked for in the number or kind of duties given us."[27] And again: "We can find all that is necessary in the present moment. We need not worry about whether to pray or be silent, whether to withdraw into retreat or mix with people, to read or write, to meditate or make our minds a receptive blank, to shun or seek out books on spirituality. Nor do poverty or riches, sickness or health, life or death matter in the least. What does matter is what each moment produces by the will of God. . . . Our only satisfaction must be to live in the present moment as if there were nothing to expect beyond it."[28]

Undoubtedly, though, the understanding of personal vocation has experienced particularly significant development in Roman Catholic circles only in the last three decades or so. Especially noteworthy is the role it plays in the thought of John Paul II. He gives a good, brief summary of the emergence of this new thinking in the following passage:

> In the period before the Second Vatican Council, the concept of "vocation" was applied first of all to the priesthood and religious life, as if Christ had addressed to the young person his evangelical "Follow me" only for these cases. The Council has broadened this way of looking at things. Priestly and religious vocations have kept their particular character and their sacramental and charismatic importance in the life of the people of God. But at the same time the awareness renewed by the Second Vatican Council of the universal sharing of all the baptized in Christ's threefold prophetic, priestly and kingly mission (*tria munera*), as also the awareness of the universal vocation to holiness, have led to a realization of the fact that every human life vocation, as a Christian vocation, corresponds to the evangelical call. Christ's "Follow me" makes

---

[27] *Abandonment to Divine Providence,* John Beevers, trans. (New York: Doubleday Image Books, 1975), 33.

[28] Ibid., 51.

itself heard on the different paths taken by the disciples and confessors of the divine Redeemer.[29]

This way of understanding individual vocation is one to which John Paul himself has made an important contribution. It is not something new for him. His book *Love and Responsibility*, which, as Karol Wojtyla, he first published in Poland in 1960, contains a succinct but insightful treatment of the subject that is helpful in the present context.[30]

The author begins with the obvious fact that vocation signifies a personal commitment; vocations are peculiar to persons. Thus "the very concept [of vocation] takes us into a very interesting and profound area of man's interior life". It is true that the call to a particular occupation or way of life often has an "external, social, and institutional" character—it comes to the person from outside, so to speak. But vocation also has a "personal and psychological" aspect that is of much great importance from a personalist perspective. "In this other meaning the word 'vocation' indicates that *there is a proper course for every person's development to follow* [emphasis in original], a specific way in which he commits his whole life to the service of certain values." Love is central to vocation understood in this way: "That a particular person has a particular vocation always . . . means that his love is fixed on some particular goal. A person who has a vocation must not only love someone but be prepared to give himself or herself for love."

Although Wojtyla clearly is not interested in only the psychological aspect of vocation, that aspect nevertheless remains crucial from his personalistic perspective even, or perhaps especially, when the religious dimension of vocation is taken into account: "An inner need to determine the main direction of one's development by love encounters an objective call

---

[29] Apostolic Letter to the Youth of the World, Mar. 31, 1985.
[30] See Karol Wojtyla, *Love and Responsibility* (New York: Farrar, Straus, Giroux, 1981), 255–58.

from God. . . . 'What is my vocation' means 'in what direction should my personality develop, considering what I have in me, what I have to offer, and what others—other people and God—expect of me?' " A religious believer knows his or her own "spiritual reserves" to be inadequate for developing the personality through love as this understanding of vocation demands. Required instead are the "operations of Grace": the individual must "learn to integrate himself into the activity of God and respond to His love".

Wojtyla speaks warmly of consecrated virginity as a "state of perfection", commended in both the New Testament and the Church's Tradition, which creates "particularly favorable conditions for the attainment of perfection in the New Testament sense". Still, he is at pains to point out, someone "living outside the 'state of perfection', but observing that greatest of commandments"—love of God above all else and love of neighbor as oneself—can be "closer to perfection than one who has chosen that state". How can that be? The answer lies in individual vocation: "In the light of the Gospel it is obvious that every man solves the problem of his vocation in practice above all by adopting a conscious personal attitude towards the supreme demand made on us in the commandment to love. This attitude is primarily a function of the person: the condition of the person—whether the person is married, celibate, or even virgin (if virginity is thought of simply as a status or a factor in the status of the person) is here of secondary importance." And so, as Pope John Paul II three decades later remarks, "The fundamental objective of the formation of the lay faithful is an ever-clearer discovery of one's vocation and the ever-greater willingness to live it so as to fulfill one's mission."[31]

Individual vocation has been an important theme in this Pope's teaching since the beginning of his pontificate. In his first encyclical, *Redemptor Hominis*, setting out his program

---

[31] *Christifideles Laici*, 58.

in general terms, he writes that although the Church can be described in the categories of the human sciences, that is not enough:

> For the whole of the community of the People of God and for each member of it what is in question is not just a specific "social membership"; rather, for each and every one what is essential is a particular "vocation". Indeed, the Church as the People of God is also—according to the teaching of Saint Paul . . . of which Pius XII reminded us in wonderful terms— "Christ's Mystical Body". Membership in that body has for its source a particular call, united with the saving action of grace. Therefore, if we wish to keep in mind this community of the People of God, which is so vast and so extremely differentiated, we must see first and foremost Christ saying in a way to each member of the community: "Follow me" [Jn 1:43]. . . . [E]very initiative serves the true renewal in the Church and helps to bring the authentic light that is Christ insofar as the initiative is based on adequate awareness of the individual Christian's vocation and of responsibility for this singular, unique and unrepeatable grace by which each Christian in the community of the People of God builds up the Body of Christ. . . . Indeed, in the Church as the community of the People of God under the guidance of the Holy Spirit's working, each member has "his own special gift", as Saint Paul teaches [1 Cor 7:7]. Although this "gift" is a personal vocation and a form of participation in the Church's saving work, it also serves others, builds the Church and the fraternal communities in the various spheres of human life on earth.[32]

And nearly a decade later, in *Christifideles Laici*, he declares:

> The fundamental objective of the formation of the lay faithful is an ever-clearer discovery of one's vocation and the ever-greater willingness to live it so as to fulfill one's mission. *God calls me and sends me forth* as a laborer in his vineyard. He calls me and sends me forth to work for the coming of

---

[32] *Redemptor Hominis*, 21.

his Kingdom in history. This personal vocation and mission define the dignity and the responsibility of each member of the lay faithful and make up the focal point of the whole work of formation, whose purpose is the joyous and grateful recognition of this dignity and the faithful and generous living-out of this responsibility.[33]

The immediate and specific standard for the Christian life of each person, each baptized member of Christ's faithful, from the Pope to the least of God's people, is set by his individual vocation. In this personalist view, the common Christian vocation provides the general framework, the basic pattern, that each one must specify precisely in the manner to which God calls him. As for state in life, it is best understood as an aspect of individual vocation, not vice versa. Thus the priesthood is the ideal, the model, for those whom their individual vocations call to it, but not for those who are not so called. The abstract superiority that may be claimed for one or another state in life or life-style is simply beside the point in this perspective. What matters in concrete fact is the answer to the question "What does God want *me* to do?"

Especially perhaps is this true of the crucial issue of personal sanctity. In this sphere, the order of Christian charity or love, even von Balthasar speaks of "a final relativization of the differences that exist among the states of life". For "it is this love that Christianity is called upon to live and to represent, and it is immaterial whether it represents it through the priestly state . . . through the lay state . . . or through the evangelical state."[34] Each of the *christifideles* is meant to pursue the unitary vocation to love within that state in life to which God's radically individualized call summons him.

It is important not to think of vocation in any of its senses merely in static terms. What is at issue here (as writers like

---

[33] *Christifideles Laici*, 58.   [34] Von Balthasar, 385–86.

Newman and De Caussade make clear) is a dynamic process—Christian life and the richly diverse lives of individual Christians—to which vocation in all its meanings gives form and specificity.

Ordinarily, though, we view Christian life and our lives as Christians in a narrow and fragmented manner. Stressing the discontinuity between life in this world and life in the next and assigning a merely instrumental value to the present life, we discount the importance of our vocations, supposing we even think of ourselves as having them, and take a minimalistic view of the fulfillment that God ultimately intends for us. (Or perhaps we simply ignore the whole question: heaven, like hell, seems mostly to have dropped out of Catholic catechesis today, as well as out of the consciousness of Catholics.)

This trivializing of human life and final human fulfillment, together with the tendency to misinterpret the link between the two, does much to create and nurture the clericalist mentality. To deal with clericalism at this level, we must start with basics.

Begin, then, with the fact that although it was impossible for God to create other beings divine by nature, inasmuch as that would have involved a contradiction (created gods), God nevertheless could and did create beings—human beings—upon whom he bestowed "grace". This grace is a participation in the divine life that makes men God's children by adoption, that is, divine by adoption.

Stated baldly, this may seem scarcely credible, but it is only what Scripture says: "Beloved, we are God's children now; it does not yet appear what we shall be, but we know that when he appears we shall be like him, for we shall see him as he is" (1 Jn 3:2); "You have been born anew, not of perishable seed but of imperishable, through the living and abiding word of God" (1 Pet 1:23); and so on. In living the life of grace, one begins to live a new, divine life. Its culmination is heaven, where, Jesus says, we shall be "sons of God . . . sons of the resurrection" (Lk 20:36).

Christian life therefore is correctly understood as a process of divinization. That also is a startling proposition when one first hears it: growing in "grace", we grow in participation in divinity. Yet this is what Fathers of the Church tell us, and it also is the teaching of Saint John of the Cross: "The tenth and last step of this secret ladder of love assimilates the soul to God completely because of the clear vision of God which a person possesses as soon as he reaches it. . . . *We know that we shall be like him* [1 Jn 3:2], not because the soul will have as much capacity as God—this is impossible—but because all that it is will become like God. Thus it will be called, and shall be, God through participation";[35] "Having been made one with God, the soul is somehow God through participation. Although it is not God as perfectly as it will be in the next life, it is like the shadow of God."[36]

Side by side with this reality we need to consider another reality taught by Vatican Council II.[37] Not only does Christian life in this world consist essentially in participation in human goods—there is, along with discontinuity, a real and momentous continuity between our participation in human goods in the present life and our fulfillment in respect to human goods in heaven. This is among the most important elements of the entire body of conciliar teaching: it opens the way to resolving the age-old conflict between life in this world and life in the next, between "the world" and "heaven", and provides the key to assigning their authentic meaning and value to human life and human endeavor.

---

[35] *The Dark Night*, vol. 2, 20, in *The Collected Works of St. John of the Cross*, Kieran Kavanaugh, O.C.D., and Otilio Rodriguez, O.C.D., trans. (Washington: Institute of Carmelite Studies, 1979), 377.

[36] *The Living Flame of Love*, 78, in *Collected Works*, 641.

[37] See *Gaudium et Spes*, 38, 39.

In discussing the diversity of the Spirit's gifts, *Gaudium et Spes* points out that some people are called to "give clear witness to the desire for a heavenly home and to keep that desire green among the human family", while others have the calling "to dedicate themselves to the earthly service of men and to make ready the material of the celestial realm by this ministry of theirs".[38] Then, in a passage of great originality and importance, the Council goes on to draw out the meaning of this notion of making ready the material of the celestial realm: here and now we are contributing to the kingdom of God—a kingdom that is already present in human history but that will reach its perfect fulfillment only in heaven.

> For after we have obeyed the Lord, and in His Spirit nurtured on earth the values of human dignity, brotherhood and freedom, and indeed all the good fruits of our nature and enterprise, we will find them again, but freed of stain, burnished and transfigured. This will be so when Christ hands over to the Father a kingdom eternal and universal: "a kingdom of truth and life, of holiness and grace, of justice, love, and peace" [Preface of the Feast of Christ the King]. On this earth that kingdom is already present in mystery. When the Lord returns, it will be brought into full flower.[39]

This marks a breakthrough at least as important as anything to be found in any of the other conciliar documents.

"Christians have very often overlooked the place which properly human goods and actions have in heavenly fulfillment", Germain Grisez writes.[40] The teaching of the Second Vatican council supplies a fundamental corrective of this oversight. It rejects the idea that human activity in the service of human goods has either merely instrumental value (do

---

[38] Ibid., 38.
[39] Ibid., 39.
[40] Germain Grisez, *The Way of the Lord Jesus*. Vol. 1, *Christian Moral Principles* (Chicago: Franciscan Herald Press, 1983), 467.

good and you will go to heaven) or exclusively immanent significance (do good simply for the sake of human betterment here and now). In place of these partial, and therefore distorted, accounts of human temporal activity, the Council offers a synthesis. For even though "earthly progress must be carefully distinguished from the growth of Christ's kingdom", still, "to the extent that the former can contribute to the better ordering of human society, it is of vital concern to the kingdom of God."[41] As Grisez says, "Little attention was paid before Vatican II to the fact that human acts last in heaven and that the blessed are fulfilled in their properly human goods. . . . [T]he Council teaches that heaven and earth are not entirely separated; the kingdom is here, though invisible, and present human acts become part of it. When the Lord returns, the moral lives Christians live in communion with his redemptive act will be completed by rich fulfillment in all the human goods: The holy will be happy."[42]

The distinctive task of the Church and her members in relation to the world is thus seen to be the *consecratio mundi*, the consecration of the world: its "restoration" to God in Christ. We shall see more of what this means shortly.

Fulfillment in respect to human goods and fulfillment in respect to divinization are not separate, distinct processes. They take place together and indeed are best understood as different aspects of one and the same process—here and now called "Christian life"—by which God acts in us and we cooperate with his acting, so that we become more and more fully and perfectly his adopted children. Commencing as it must in the present life, this process is completed in the life of heaven.

It is helpful to see baptism in this light. It unites us with Jesus; and, since he is God, it serves as a kind of birth into

---

[41] *Gaudium et Spes*, 39.

[42] Grisez, *The Way of the Lord Jesus*, 468.

the new life by which those who are baptized become, as it were, God's embryonic offspring.[43] Another way of expressing this is to say that baptism effects our incorporation into Christ and into his Mystical Body, the community of Faith: "By the sacrament of baptism . . . a man becomes truly incorporated into the crucified and glorified Christ and is reborn to a sharing of the divine life. . . . Baptism, therefore, constitutes a sacramental bond of unity linking all who have been reborn by means of it."[44] Other sacraments do not add anything extrinsic to baptism but are particular ways of unfolding and specifying what is already essentially, though implicitly, there. The Eucharist in particular carries incorporation into Christ further in a unique and extraordinary manner; sustaining and intensifying our identification with Jesus, it more than anything else helps Christians to "put on Christ", have "the mind of Christ", become integrally "Christlike", not merely by imitation but specifically by bodily communion.

Baptism also is the source of the common Christian vocation, the calling to cooperate in and continue the work of Jesus that is common to all his disciples: "It is no exaggeration to say that the entire existence of the lay faithful has as its purpose to lead a person to a knowledge of the radical newness of the Christian life that comes from Baptism, the sacrament of faith, so that this knowledge can help that person live the responsibilities which arise from that vocation received from God. . . . Thus with the outpouring of the Holy Spirit in Baptism and Confirmation, the baptized share in the same mission of Jesus as the Christ, the Savior-Messiah."[45]

More specifically, this common vocation, shared by lay members of the Church along with the rest, is a participation in what is traditionally understood as the triple ministry that

---

[43] Jn 3:3–6; cf. Grisez, *The Way of the Lord Jesus*, 737–38.
[44] Vatican II, *Unitatis Redintegratio*, 22.
[45] *Christifideles Laici*, 10, 13.

is properly Jesus'. Citing the First Epistle of Peter (2:4–5, 9), Pope John Paul remarks; "A new aspect of the grace and dignity coming from Baptism is here introduced: the lay faithful participate, for their part, in the threefold mission of Christ as Priest, Prophet and King."[46]

We have already seen how Vatican II and *Christifideles Laici* view the content of these three roles as they apply to members of the Church, particularly laymen. Here it is important to underline the fact that the idea of vocation is essential to making sense of Christian life in general as well as comprehending one's individual life as a Christian. The alternative to seeing oneself as called by God is to interpret one's various roles and duties, including membership in the Church herself, as mere arbitary facts—accidents of personal history, offshoots of personal taste and inclination, circumstances to be manipulated as suits one's advantage.

It is true of course that even for someone who sees his ecclesial role as a vocation, personal choice—a commitment to that vocation, reaffirmed when necessary against temptations to abandon it, and countless subsequent specific decisions to do what is necessary to carry out the commitment thus undertaken—remains indispensable: in no sense does "vocation" signify passivity in the one called. But by introducing God into the picture, the idea of vocation removes the curse of arbitrariness from life. In speaking of one's ecclesial vocation, whether as a priest, a religious, or a layman, one is speaking of one's part in God's redemptive plan.

By baptism, then, laymen, along with all the other members of the Church, share in the mission of Christ, which is also the Church's mission; confirmation "confirms" this calling and gives it its specific orientation to apostolate. This can be expressed in many ways, but, as suggested earlier, one that is both traditional and evocative is to speak of the *consecratio mundi*, the consecration of the world: in other words,

[46] Ibid., 14.

the carrying-out of God's plan "to unite all things in him [Christ]".[47] Of the laity Pope John Paul says that "in ordering creation to the authentic well-being of humanity in an activity governed by the life of grace, they share in the exercise of the power with which the Risen Christ draws all things to himself and subjects them along with himself to the Father, so that God might be everything to everyone (cf. 1 Cor 15:28; Jn 12:32)".[48] For laymen, however, the *consecratio mundi* has a specifically, properly secular character; it is expressed by Christian humanism lived out in the world.

Because it has its source in the baptismal vocation common to every member of the Church, this participation by the laity in the Church's mission does not depend upon a hierarchical mandate. It belongs intrinsically to laymen by inherent duty and right. Plainly this is true of personal apostolate—what individual laymen do on their own initiative in order to further the cause of religion and serve others—but it is no less true of groups of laity who come together for Christian action on an organized basis. Thus the Code of Canon Law affirms that "Christ's faithful may freely establish and direct associations which serve charitable or pious purposes or which foster the christian vocation in the world" (Canon 215).

Lay people, as the Catholic Action model correctly pointed out and as ceremonies of institution into lay ministries now remind us, do require a hierarchical mandate to participate in the work proper to the clerical hierarchy. As John Paul II remarks, "the task exercised in virtue of supply"—that is, clerics' work done by laity where there are not enough clerics to do it—"takes its legitimacy formally and immediately from the official deputation given by the pastors, as well as from its concrete exercise under the guidance of ecclesiastical authority".[49]

[47] Eph 1:10.
[48] *Christifideles Laici*, 14.
[49] Ibid., 23.

But it is very different with the apostolate proper to laymen. Canon 216 is clear and specific: "Since they share in the Church's mission, all Christ's faithful have the right to promote and support apostolic action, by their own initiative, undertaken according to their state and condition." (The canon does, however, add that "no initiative . . . can lay claim to the title 'catholic' without the consent of the competent ecclesiastical authority." Laymen cannot commit the Church on their own, as in fact few would either claim or wish to do.)

In speaking of "the apostolate that is proper to lay people", we are speaking of vocation in its second large sense or meaning: that is, vocation understood as covering any state in life—cleric, religious, layman. And as we have seen, it is a tangled question (into which I have no intention of entering here) just which life-styles ought properly to be designated as "states in life". What is relevant for our purposes is that by God's will the common, baptismal vocation is specified more particularly by the various states and generic life-styles to which individuals are called. So, holy orders specifies the baptismal vocation for clerics, while matrimony specifies the baptismal vocation for the married laity.

In order that the Church's comprehensive mission may be carried on integrally, diverse states in life and Christian life-styles must make their special contributions. The Church is the Body of Christ, and all her members are needed for her to function as she should: "If all were a single organ, where would the body be? As it is, there are many parts, yet one body. The eye cannot say to the hand, 'I have no need of you', nor again the head to the feet, 'I have no need of you'. On the contrary, the parts of the body which seem to be weaker are indispensable."[50] If, however, states in life and Christian life-styles do in fact have the character of vocation—a calling from God—there simply are no rational

[50] 1 Cor 12:19–22.

grounds for elitism or envy among members of the Church: not just because these attitudes are excluded on ethical grounds but also because they have no basis in reality.

As for the specific relationship between the baptismal priesthood of the faithful and the ordained priesthood, the difference in kind, not just in degree, to which Vatican II calls attention, is based upon the specific empowerment of the ordained priest enabling him to function as sacramental proxy for Christ in certain of the sacraments, in particular the Eucharist. We shall have reason to consider the implications of this at greater length below. Here it is sufficient to say that, more than just supporting the distinction between priest and people, this difference in kind is required by their complementarity. The nonordained and the ordained, people and priest, need one another in order to be fully themselves as ecclesial beings.[51]

And finally, of course, it is imperative that vocation also be understood and appreciated as *individual* vocation: the special calling by which God summons each member of the Church to play a unique role in his redemptive plan and therefore in the Church's mission. By reason of their baptism, all the members of the Church, the *christifideles,* enjoy a radical equality and are meant to participate in the Church's work; but in functional terms they are distinguished from one another not just by being called to diverse states in life but also, more immediately, by their unique individual vocations, of which "state in life" is only one element.

Implied in all this is an understanding of the Church that views her as a setting for complementary actions by *christifideles* of various ranks and conditions, all contributing to her mission by living not only their common baptismal vocation but also their several state in life vocations and their countless individual vocations. At least since Vatican II, the preferred

---

[51] "The Priestly Ministry", in Sharkey, 52.

model for expressing this ideal situation has been that of the Church as *communio,* a community or communion of persons. It offers many advantages for realizing the vocational schema presented here. At its heart is the idea of a union of human persons, in a manner that fully respects their individual identities, both with the Divine Persons and with one another: in this understanding, the Church can be thought of as a kind of extended family.

This means that one who is baptized is fundamentally neither a cleric nor a layman but a member of Christ and therefore a member of Christ's priestly people. The testimony of the New Testament is clear: "[I]n Christ Jesus you are all sons of God, through faith. For as many of you as were baptized into Christ have put on Christ. There is neither Jew nor Greek, there is neither slave nor free, there is neither male nor female; for you are all one in Christ Jesus."[52] Such radical devaluing of distinctions extends far beyond the level of sociological categories. It is based precisely upon the new relationship that the baptized have to Christ and also, as a consequence, upon their new relationships with one another deriving from this primordial relationship to the one whom, in baptism, all equally have "put on".

Thus this devaluing of distinctions—which implies, positively, an affirmation of equality and unity—expresses a specifically ecclesial and evangelical reality of immense significance: those who are baptized into Christ receive both a new individual identity and a new *corporate* identity and, with these, a new mission: "But you are a chosen race, a royal priesthood, a holy nation, God's own people, that you may declare the wonderful deeds of him who called you out of darkness into his marvellous light."[53] The central meaning is clear. The fundamental category of membership in the Church—of engrafting into Christ—is not layman or cleric or religious. It is *christifidelis.*

[52] Gal 3:26–28.   [53] 1 Pet 2:9.

Strongly emphasized by the Council, this point has important practical consequences. For example: "[A]ll persons who belong to the Church have a common fundamental legal status, because they share one and the same basic theological condition and belong to the same primary common category." It therefore follows that

> all the faithful, from the Pope to the child who has just been baptized, share one and the same vocation, the same faith, the same Spirit, the same grace. They are all in need of appropriate sacramental and spiritual aids; they must all live a full Christian life, following the same evangelical teachings; they must all lead a basic personal life of piety—that of children of God, brothers and disciples of Christ—which is obligatory for them before and above any specific distinctions which may arise from their different functions within the Church. They all have an active and appropriate share—within the inevitable plurality of ministries—in the single mission of Christ and of the Church.[54]

Within the *communio* model are at least two submodels, as it were, expressing different but complementary realities about the ecclesial community. One, closely identified with Vatican II, is the Church as people of God.[55] The other, elaborated even before the Council by Pope Pius XII, is the Church as the Mystical Body of Christ.[56] There is no question of choosing between the two. The operative principle here is complementarity: each of these images of the Church says something essential about the Church's complex reality.

To speak of the Church as people of God calls attention to the radical subordination of all the *christifideles* to God and their radical equality and unity with one another: "Christ the Lord, High Priest taken from among men (cf. Heb 5:1–5), 'made a kingdom and priests to God his Father' (Rev

---

[54] Del Portillo, 19.
[55] See *Lumen Gentium*, 9–17.
[56] See encyclical letter *Mystici Corporis* (1943).

1:6; cf. 5:9–10) out of this new people. The baptized, by regeneration and the anointing of the Holy Spirit, are consecrated into a spiritual house and a holy priesthood."[57] Likewise, to speak of the Church as the Body of Christ calls attention to her hierarchical structure, as fully intended by Jesus as the radical equality of the members: "For the nurturing and constant growth of the People of God, Christ the Lord instituted in His Church a variety of ministries, which work for the good of the whole body. For those ministers who are endowed with sacred power are servants of their brethren, so that all who are of the People of God, and therefore enjoy a true Christian dignity, can work toward a common goal freely and in an orderly way, and arrive at salvation."[58]

The *communio* model encompasses all of these dimensions of the Church's reality: subordination to God and union with him, radical equality and hierarchical ordering of the members. In so doing, it is of central importance to contemporary efforts to extricate the Church from the dead ends of clericalism and neocongregationalism. Thus the entire second chapter of *Christifideles Laici* is devoted to an extended treatment of "The Participation of the Lay Faithful in the Life of the Church as Communion". John Paul II writes of ecclesial communion that "at one and the same time it is characterized by a *diversity* and a *complementarity* of vocations and states in life, of ministries, of charisms and responsibilities. Because of this diversity and complementarity every member of the lay faithful is seen *in relation to the whole body* and offers a *totally unique contribution* on behalf of the whole body."[59]

Even so, up to now a great deal of the Church's postconciliar history has been a record of conflicts and power struggles, often arising either from clericalist attitudes and assumptions or from extreme reactions against these. "Either each person and each community is church . . ." begins a recent exposi-

---

[57] *Lumen Gentium*, 10.
[58] Ibid., 18.
[59] *Christifideles Laici*, 20.

tion of radical neocongregationalism. But who really needs to finish that particular sentence? If each person and each community really is church, then the possibility of the Church as a universal communion has collapsed under the weight of an individualistic and centrifugal ecclesiology.

Sometimes the idea of people of God has itself been perverted by being interpreted politically, as if it signified the democratization of the Church. It is important in this context to be aware of the Old Testament roots of the idea. It is founded upon covenant—God is Lord and takes this people under his protection, makes it his own—so that the community-forming act is *not* some kind of social contract among the members of the community themselves; it is God's revelation and his offer of covenant.[60] While there is no excuse for the nervous defensiveness exhibited by conservative, clericalist ecclesiastics in reaction to reasonable suggestions for introducing democratic ways into ecclesial life where they fit, neither is there any excuse for simplistic, ideologically motivated efforts at radical democratization based on the false claim that these somehow reflect Vatican II's ecclesiology. (The "people's Church" cherished by romantic liberationists comes to mind.)

"It is not the promotion of this trend [false democratization] but *communio* as fruit and dynamic impetus of the Holy Spirit that needs to be kept in view", according to Bishop Paul Josef Cordes of the Pontifical Council for the Laity. And he adds, citing Saint Paul: "Whoever claims to be filled with the Spirit will not want to stand on the sidelines of the Church."[61]

But are not the sidelines precisely where clericalist attitudes, even in concealed form, still force many to remain? And, to pursue the metaphor, do not the solutions to this problem

---

[60] See *Lumen Gentium*, 9.   [61] Cordes, 181–82.

proposed by neocongregationalism amount to telling all the players to compete for the same position instead of working together as a team?

The elements for making an end of clericalism now exist. They are a new theology of vocation that emphasizes unique individual vocation, a new vision of Christian life that stresses the continuity in human goods between life in this world and life in heaven, and a new ecclesiology of the Church as *communio*. The challenge we face is to put these principles to work.

VI

BEYOND CLERICALISM

I have not set out to write a book prescribing new programs for the Church to rid herself of clericalism. Programs can be helpful, but something else is more important. Clericalism is essentially a matter of attitude and mind-set: it will not be corrected by forming a committee, setting up an office, publishing a newsletter, and seeking foundation grants. Its permanent removal from Catholic life will come about only by change of heart—conversion.

But it *is* possible to do things that will make conversion either more or less likely. Simply from that perspective, I draw this discussion to a close with some reflections on specifics, including public opinion in the Church, clerical celibacy and the ordination of married men to the priesthood, the relationship between the laity and the clergy and the role of each in the Church's overall mission, lay ministries, and the treatment due laymen who work for the Church.

Despite the endorsement given to the *communio* model of the Church by Vatican II and subsequent magisterial teaching, the structures needed to realize it in practice either remain seriously underdeveloped or else do not exist at all. This is true, for example, of public opinion in the Church.

There are many official testimonials to its value. The Council speaks of the need for public opinion in its Dogmatic

Constitution on the Church.[1] The postconciliar Pastoral Instruction on Social Communications declares: "Since the Church is a living body, she needs public opinion in order to sustain a giving and taking between her members. Without this, she cannot advance in thought and action. 'Something would be lacking in her life if she had no public opinion. Both pastors of souls and lay people would be to blame for this' [Pope Pius XII, allocution of February 17, 1950]."[2] Canon 212.3 of the revised Code of Canon Law elevates such observations to the level of general law: "[Christ's faithful] have the right, indeed at times the duty, in keeping with their knowledge, competence and position, to manifest to the sacred Pastors their views on matters which concern the good of the Church. They have the right to make their views known to others of Christ's faithful."

In speaking of public opinion, Vatican II encourages the laity to express their views "through the agencies set up by the Church for this purpose".[3] What are these? A Catholic can always write a letter to a pastor or bishop and hope it will do some good; the Catholic press provides a limited forum for expressing opinions and exchanging ideas; and in a number of places since the Council, conscientious efforts have been made to establish and sustain advisory bodies like diocesan and parish pastoral councils on which laymen serve. Even the departments of the Holy See have adopted structures and processes for consultation in which qualified laymen take part.

Still, it seems safe to say that many ordinary Catholics feel they have no real access to any effective mechanism for expressing their views to the pastors of the Church. For many others, due to their passivity in religious matters, the question simply does not arise. As we saw earlier, the U.S. diocesan

---

[1] See *Lumen Gentium*, 37.
[2] *Communio et Progressio*, 115.
[3] *Lumen Gentium*, 37.

responses to the Vatican survey before the 1987 Synod of Bishops on the laity took note of this oppressive reality.

Perhaps the blame rests with these inert laymen; they neglect to make use of the structures and processes of public opinion that already exist. Leaving aside the question of blame, however, the fact is that not a few Catholics, including not a few who do practice their religion, have to a great extent lost interest in the Church because they think the Church has no real interest in them—at least, not as autonomous, competent individuals capable of contributing something (besides money) if allowed to do so. A situation like this, in which the ideal of public opinion is commended in principle but not realized in practice, can only contribute to the apathy, alienation, frustration, and tension already existing within the Church.

But let us not simply leave it at that. Despite the many problems it creates, the paucity of structures and processes for the expression of public opinion in the Church during the last quarter-century has on balance probably been a blessing. Considering the pervasiveness of the clericalist mindset among not only clerics but also, perhaps especially, laymen, the result of doing more to create such structures and processes in the years since the Council very likely would have been an even greater institutionalization of clericalism, although now with an approved veneer of "renewal" as envisioned by liberal Catholics.

This is not a fanciful worry. As far back as 1964, Daniel Callahan was lamenting the fact that "there is nothing yet in the *structure* of the Church which provides for the guaranteed continuation of this permissiveness, this creative listening on the part of the hierarchy which we are now experiencing."[4] How often since then have the Pope and bishops been exhorted to engage in "creative listening" and excoriated for not listen-

---

[4] Callahan, in Murray, 165.

ing as creatively as they should? This has been one of the great ecclesiastical scams of the era. For much of the talk about "listening" and about the need to create structures for public opinion has been aimed at immobilizing the Magisterium in the exercise of its function of judging and teaching.

Back in the early 1970s, the pros and cons of creating a National Pastoral Council for the Church in the United States were seriously debated in some churchy circles. Although nothing came of the idea, it seems clear that, whatever the merits of the scheme might have been in principle (or might yet prove to be if it is revived in the future), any such body as a National Pastoral Council established in those years would have been dominated by clericalized liberal cadres—priests, religious, and laymen—who even today compose much of the bureaucratic and academic middle management of American Catholicism and, in that role, seek to bend the Magisterium according to their version of what is good for the Church.

This program in its essence was spread on the record as a result of another venture of that period, the Call to Action conference of 1976. Views of that gathering and of who was responsible for it still vary. I recall standing just after the conference had ended with a group of bishops outside a hotel in downtown Detroit, waiting for a chartered bus to come and take us to the airport. "Why do you staff people in Washington make things like this happen?" one of them asked me angrily. "Why do you bishops let them happen?" I replied.

The Call to Action proposals, a mixed bag ranging from the unexceptionable (condemnations of racism and the arms race) to the outrageous (tendentious declarations on such issues as women's ordination, divorce and remarriage, birth control, and homosexuality), added up to an agenda of liberal activism in the political arena and pluralistic permissiveness within the Church; the idea was that the bishops should put it all obediently into effect. But despite the conference's power-to-the-people atmospherics, typical of the pseudo-revolutionary playacting in that heady era, the recommendations were actually the work of a body of participants "a majority of whom were employed by church agencies".[5] There is no meaningful sense in which such a group could be described as representative of anything except the preoccupations and prejudices of liberal clericalism.

The Administrative Committee of the National Conference of Catholic Bishops, seemingly abashed by the outcome of this highly publicized exercise carried out under episcopal auspices, delicately alluded to this embarrassing circumstance in a statement some six months later: "Admittedly, the process of consultation was imperfect. . ."[6]

Although there has been no exact repetition of the experiment since then, even today the Call to Action is more than just a yellowed page in ecclesiastical history. For as the commentator quoted above, a Call to Action planner and supporter, points out, the process employed on this occasion gave important impetus to the practice of consultation, which has become common in the Church in the United States since then.[7]

It is a good and desirable thing in principle that the pastors consult. What better way to ascertain the state of public sentiment and do what Newman a century and a half ago commended as useful, even necessary, for the health of the Church? Unfortunately, in many cases the national and local consultations carried out in recent years by the American bishops have mainly involved clerics, religious, and laymen closely linked to the Church bureaucracy and steeped in clericalist interests and attitudes. Most Catholics have never been seriously consulted by their bishops about anything, and some who have volunteered opinions to their pastoral leaders have been sharply rebuked for doing so.

---

[5] David O'Brien, *Public Catholicism* (New York: Macmillan, 1989), 244.

[6] "The Bicentennial Consultation: A Response to the Call to Action", in Nolan, vol. 4, 215.

[7] O'Brien, 244.

Some of this may be unavoidable. Bishops cannot *force* anyone to take part in a consultative process, and by and large only those who are interested will spontaneously come forward. Usually, this means people with ideological axes to grind or personal interests to promote. In the present context, however, the result is that consultation in the Church typically consists in soliciting predictable opinions from activists and professional or semiprofessional Church workers. That not only calls into question the value of such consultation but also underlines the indifference and passivity prevailing among a vast body of laymen, who themselves take the view—so painfully typical of a clericalized laity—that what happens in and to the Church is no concern of theirs.

Other questions, not unrelated to clericalism, also must be asked about consultation in the Church as it is currently practiced.

For example: Given the circumstances of the Catholic community in the United States today, what is the purpose of consulting laymen on ecclesial matters? To obtain exact information about the state of a more or less disordered public opinion resulting from secularization and cultural assimilation, catechetical neglect, theological dissent, and a series of wrenching ecclesiastical controversies, as a step toward finding and applying remedies? (If so, scientific polling would do the job better than amateur pulse-taking organized by Church bureaucrats.) To fill in gaps in the pastors' own knowledge and insight? (Personal contact with people in less structured settings would be preferable.) To perform a ritual demanded by today's preferred nonauthoritarian leadership style, with a view to enlisting public support for the leaders' decisions? (Not unreasonable, but more manipulative than most nonauthoritarian leaders are willing to admit.) Something else?

It is questionable whether those who now routinely practice consultation in the Church have thought about exactly why they are doing it. Moreover, the results of many consultations are skewed and invalidated by the fact that those who participate are mainly representative of the views of liberal clericalism. And so the paradox of the present moment: we need structures for consultation and the expression of public opinion in the Church, but the persistence of clericalism tends to vitiate such structures and processes as exist. The solution is not to do away with consultation and forget about public opinion. It is to do away with clericalism, so that an authentic public opinion, honestly expressed and responsibly but not slavishly heeded by the authorities, can begin to emerge in the Church.

The interlocking series of problems revolving around public opinion and consultation points to an underlying reality of great practical importance. Clericalism stands as an obstacle to addressing and dealing realistically with many issues and concerns in Catholic life; it is the invisible roadblock preventing the authentic renewal of the Church. That is so, for example, with the question of clerical celibacy, so hotly debated for so many years and now apparently destined for even closer scrutiny as the shortage of priests grows more acute.

There is a compelling case for celibacy. Vatican II sums it up in its document on the priesthood: "Through virginity or celibacy observed for the sake of the kingdom of heaven, priests are consecrated to Christ in a new and distinguished way. They more easily hold fast to Him with undivided heart. They more freely devote themselves in Him and through Him to the service of God and men. They more readily minister to His kingdom and to the work of heavenly regeneration, and thus become more apt to exercise paternity in Christ, and do so to a greater extent." And in addition there is the eschatological witness of celibacy: "[Priests] become a vivid sign of that future world which is already present through faith and charity."[8]

Not only is this a beautiful ideal, it is an ideal that has been realized in the lives of innumerable celibate priests of

[8] *Presbyterorum Ordinis*, 16.

the past and present. But there is another side to the coin. It is clerical bachelorhood as an adjunct of clericalism—an important element in the caste system that divides priests from laymen, a kind of ticket of admission to a clerical club and the privileges it offers to those who are willing and able to pay for them. "What privileges?" someone might ask. Automatic social status, a standard of living that frequently surpasses that of lay parishioners, a schedule no more demanding than a man might care to impose on himself, little professional supervision and accountability, lifetime job security—these things come to mind.

At the same time, as priests in recent years have generously surrendered many of the privileges previously associated with clerical elitism, or the privileges have simply drained away in the face of changing social and ecclesiastical circumstances, the price of the ticket, celibacy, has become unacceptably dear in the eyes of many persons. Hence celibacy's present status as a "problem", that is, a factor in the low morale of some priests and also in the falloff in new priestly vocations. All this is part of the legacy of clericalism.

Both the mind-set of clericalism and today's radical reactions against it attach distorted meanings to priestly celibacy. In doing so, they complicate the task of forming an accurate estimation of celibacy and valuing it properly. Here, too, a thoroughly satisfactory solution to the "problem" of celibacy will remain out of reach until the Church comes to grips with clericalism and its offspring.[9]

---

[9] Is celibacy a factor in the recent rash of sex scandals involving some clerics and religious? Plainly, not celibacy as such. As for clerical bachelorhood, imperfectly accepted and poorly lived out—I would not care to hazard a guess. Still, it is not difficult to imagine detecting a certain clericalist arrogance behind some of this behavior. It is as if the perpetrators were to say, "Of course the rules that apply to other people—laymen, that is—do not apply to me", while the clerical authorities have sometimes managed to give the impression of being more solicitous to protect the perpetrators than those, usually laity, of whom they have taken advantage.

Much the same might be said of the suggestion that, in response to the growing shortage of celibate clergy, qualified married men should be ordained as priests to celebrate the Eucharist and perform other sacramental functions in their parishes. Although Pope John Paul is adamantly opposed to the idea, its discussion will continue, for better or worse. It is important, then, that the ordination of married men *not* be viewed merely as a stopgap response to the priest shortage, since that approach could be counted on to create a new caste system *within* the priesthood: celibates as full-time "real" priests, married men as part-time "substitute" clergy.

Instead, the idea of ordaining married men should be weighed on its intrinsic merits, something that clericalism now makes nearly impossible. Apart from the risk of creating a new caste system within the priesthood, the great danger in adopting this practice lies in the possibility that it would further clericalize the laity by reinforcing the notion that committed men (and women?) seek ordination, while those who are lukewarm and selfish settle for the lay condition. To get over this hurdle, if it ever comes to that, we must first get over the hurdle of clericalism and its elitist assumptions about the superiority of the clerical state.

The most useful thing that those who wish to argue for the ordination of married men could do now would be to find out what the experience of a married clergy has been among Eastern Catholics, the Orthodox, Anglicans, and Protestants. Does ordaining married men tend to dispel clericalist attitudes or reinforce them? It is irresponsible for Catholics in the Western Church to debate this matter without learning from the experience of others.

Even more serious for its implications beyond the ecclesial community is the confusion that now surrounds a basic question concerning Catholic laymen: Which is more important, their role in the Church or their role in the secular world? Is the lay vocation a calling to staff ecclesiastical structures and programs or to serve secular institutions and the cause of human progress, contributing to human betterment not apart from the gospel but precisely in its light?

When the question is put in those terms, the answer is clear. The specific ecclesial role of a layman *includes* his role in the secular world, provided this is understood and accepted as an element in his secular vocation; but that does not *exclude* work within the structures of the Church for those whose individual vocations lead them that way.

A "secular quality", Vatican II remarks, is "proper and special" to laymen; "the laity by their very vocation, seek the kingdom of God by engaging in temporal affairs and by ordering them according to the plan of God."[10] Time and again the Council hammers at this point. The laity, it insists, are "bound to penetrate the world with a Christian spirit"; they are "called to be witnesses to Christ in all things in the midst of human society".[11] Laymen "must take on the renewal of the temporal order as their own special obligation".[12] In doing so, they are not to act under clerical direction and control, not to function as the long arm of the hierarchy. Rather, they are to carry out their tasks autonomously: "As citizens they must cooperate with other citizens, using their own special skills and acting on their own responsibility."[13]

Who would argue with that today? It is conventional wisdom. At the same time, nevertheless, we need to take into account—as these sweeping prescriptions for the laity do not— the practical implications of individual vocation. Although it is true that laymen are called to work in the world and clerics in the Church, Vatican II also reasonably recognizes exceptions to the general rule. Thus "those in holy orders can at times engage in secular activities and even have a secular profession";[14] while the Council exhorts pastors "confidently

---

[10] *Lumen Gentium*, 31.
[11] *Gaudium et Spes*, 43.
[12] *Apostolicam Actuositatem*, 7.
[13] Ibid.
[14] *Lumen Gentium*, 31.

[to] assign duties to [the layman] in the service of the Church, allowing him freedom and room for action".[15] The secular order is properly but not exclusively the laity's sphere of action, the world of ecclesiastical structures properly but not exclusively the priest's.

Even so, the general rule holds. Through the lay apostolate—"a participation in the saving mission of the Church itself"—laymen are "called in a special way to make the Church present and operative in those places and circumstances where only through them can she become the salt of the earth".[16]

Clericalism makes a grievous muddle of all this. Historically, the monastic-clericalist mentality has regarded the secular order with deep suspicion and devalued the enterprises and activities of lay Christians there. Marriage, family life, work, secular pursuits in general—no doubt laymen are required to attend to such matters. But they reek of compromise: these are needful but inglorious concessions to human weakness. By contrast, truly generous followers of Christ, people who crave to love and serve God above all else, will shun worldly entanglements and seek perfection in the clerical or religious state. That laymen do not do this ipso facto condemns them to inferior status as Christians.

Measured against an adequate understanding of vocation in its three-dimensional complexity (baptismal vocation, state in life or special service vocation, individual vocation), this manner of thinking plainly fails in at least two respects: it does not grasp the implications of *individual* calling, and it makes an a priori assumption that the monastic-clerical condition sets the ideal standard for everyone. But that is wrong. In practical terms, any particular state in life, any Christian life-style, provides the normative model only for those whom God calls to it. A Christian who recognizes that it is God's will that he live as a layman and be a spouse, parent, and worker responds precisely as God wants by seeking to realize

[15] Ibid., 38.   [16] Ibid., 33.

his individual vocation in the lay state through the commitments of marriage, family life, secular occupation, citizenship, and so on. At the very least, such a person would be making things more difficult (even, in a sense, more difficult for God) by rejecting a true vocation in favor of pursuing the supposedly "higher" vocation of a priest or religious. No doubt there are malcontents among the laity who missed their callings to be priests, but are there not also priests and religious who missed their callings as laymen because they took all too literally the message of clerical elitism that the lay condition is for the second-rate?

Today, this ancient source of misunderstanding not only coexists with the decline in priestly and religious vocations but also contributes to it by discouraging people who feel no immediate attraction to the priesthood or religious life from engaging in vocational discernment. The assumption is that someone who does not feel called to be a priest or religious does not have a vocation. But if every member of the Church took it for granted that, as a matter of fact, he *does* have a vocation, a true personal calling from God carrying with it a pressing obligation to respond, the discernment process itself would lead many to the discovery that, after all, God *has* called them to the priesthood or religious life; while discernment would uncover to the rest the particulars of their unique individual vocations as laymen living in the world.

Adding to the current confusion is the proliferation of lay ministries.

Plainly there are room and need for lay ministries in the Church. The opening, or reopening, of certain ministerial roles to laymen is one of the positive achievements since Vatican II.

But "ministries" are not the essential and proper ecclesial work of the laity. The unintended bad results of overemphasizing them are now becoming increasingly visible in symptoms like these: the use of the term "ministry" to refer to any Church-related role or activity that someone wishes to encourage, the recruitment of laymen to do clerics' work when clerics are available to do it, the emergence among some lay ministers of an elitist spirit and an unhealthy interest in ecclesiastical power, the persistence of apathy and noninvolvement on the part of the great mass of the laity, and confusion among some priests concerning their identity and role.[17]

To repeat: the emergence of lay ministries in and of itself is a commendable development. "I am convinced", a supporter writes, "that these primarily lay ministries are bringing tremendous new life, talents and energy to our churches and that women especially are in the forefront of these good changes."[18] By all means, let us welcome and encourage lay ministries.

But not without sober recognition of the ambiguities and the risks: "Yes, lay ministries by all means, but . . ." There are reasons for that hesitation.

Some of these need not detain us long. It is said, for example, that lay ministries tend to heighten the uncertainty and insecurity of priests, and there is no reason to dispute the statement. As more and more laymen perform functions like distributing Communion and doing liturgical readings, which formerly were reserved to clerics, some of the latter begin to ask what is distinctive about their ministry.

But what are we to make of that questioning? It is hard to swallow the notion that lay eucharistic ministers and lay lectors represent a threat to a secure, well-balanced priest. If there is a crisis of priestly identity today—and apparently there is—its roots surely go deeper than *that,* in which case lay ministries may actually be helping to resolve this crisis

---

[17] On the impact of lay ministries upon priests, see Committee on Priestly Life and Ministry, National Conference of Catholic Bishops, "Reflections on the Morale of Priests", *Origins* 18, no. 31, Jan. 12, 1989.

[18] Edward C. Sellner, "Lay Leadership in the 1990's", *America*, Sept. 9–16, 1989.

by forcing an overdue rethinking of ministry in general and ordained ministry in particular.

Clericalist props *should* be removed from thinking about the ordained priesthood so that a sounder way of thinking can emerge. If the rethinking occasioned in part by lay ministries contributes to this, lay ministries will have performed a useful service to priests as well as laity, even though it be at the cost of some temporary confusion.

Another worry often noted in discussions of lay ministry has to do with the danger of clericalizing laymen—distracting them from their specific and proper apostolate in and to the secular order in favor of a role *within* Church structures and based upon the clericalist view of vocation. For example, Pope John Paul points out that, even though the 1987 Synod had many positive things to say about lay ministries, it also brought to the surface some matters of concern, including "the tendency towards a 'clericalization' of the lay faithful".[19]

There are no data to show the dimensions of this problem. Considering how pervasive the clericalist mentality is among lay Catholics as well as among the clergy, one can reasonably suppose that lay ministry can and does contribute to the clericalization of some laymen. But in the absence of information on the extent of the problem, it is best to proceed very slowly in aiming pejorative epithets—"clericalist", "clericalized"—at laymen who are active in ministries. Their fundamental impulse is a generous one, and in many places they now render useful, even indispensable, service. In such circumstances it is best simply to note the danger of clericalization and let it go at that.

At the same time, however, two related problems need to be taken very seriously.

The first concerns the danger that lay ministries will foster a new, clerical-elitist caste system *among* the laymen in parishes, with the ministers regarded as the active, committed

---

[19] *Christifideles Laici*, 23.

elite and the rest of the laity, including even some who are much involved in parish life, considered inferior.

Are the CYO coaches, the people who run parish socials, the choir members, the parishioners who patiently direct parking lot traffic before and after Sunday Masses, and the rest of the small army of women and men who make any moderately large and busy parish work, really doing less to build and sustain the community of Faith than those who help distribute Communion and do liturgical readings? It would be hard to prove that they are—but the rhetoric of lay ministries sometimes implies as much.

A related problem concerns the impact that too much emphasis on lay ministry, or the wrong kind of emphasis, has on the view that people who are *not* ministers take toward their secular responsibilities. If the message is that exemplary, active, involved laity necessarily express their religious commitment through ministry (in other words, "ministry" is the standard by which to measure today's Catholic layman, much as the clericalist mentality took priesthood as the standard in an earlier day), what does that say to the great mass of laymen who are not attracted to ministry and probably never will be?

It says many things, but among them is this: "When push comes to shove, what you laymen do in 'the world' isn't terribly important in religious terms. Laity who wish to do what the Church asks of them get involved in lay ministries so that they can do some of the things that only priests used to do. As for those of you who *don't*—the Church doesn't expect much of you, and you needn't expect much of yourselves."

It will be clear, I trust, that these are not arguments against lay ministries as such but only against the kind of false emphases and misunderstandings that can, but need not, accompany their entry into the mainstream of Catholic life. As the number of priests and religious in the United States falls in the years immediately ahead, the number of lay ministers almost certainly will rise and their visibility will increase. This is inevitable and, especially in these circumstances, desirable. But as it happens it would be tragic if one unintended result were to give a new lease on life to clericalist thinking. To prevent that, it is important to avoid the sort of unreflective boosterism that exalts lay ministry while denigrating the apostolate of the laity in and to the secular world.

Finally, concern for the well-being of lay ministry itself requires addressing certain tangled questions reflected in the pages of *Christifideles Laici*. On the one hand, Pope John Paul speaks there of ministries that come from baptism and confirmation (distinguishing these from ministry that comes from the sacrament of orders); on the other hand, he insists that the exercise of lay ministries be validated by "official deputation given by the pastors".[20]

There is no problem with this—on the contrary, it makes good sense—if the deputation of lay ministers by the pastors of the Church is understood as a practical measure intended to forestall chaotic situations in which enthusiasts might take it upon themselves to engage in formal ministries on their own initiative. That would violate the Church's hierarchical structure and fracture her unity. But there is a problem if "deputation" is understood as a necessary condition for the very existence of a call to lay ministry, since this seems difficult to reconcile with the idea that lay ministries arise immediately from baptism and confirmation.

The issue comes down to this: Are laymen, by virtue of baptism and confirmation, ipso facto called to ministry (even though the pastors of the Church have their own right and duty to regulate and control the exercise of lay ministries for the good of the community as a whole), or is some form of hierarchical deputation essential to this calling (much as Catholic Action insisted that laymen had to receive a hierarchical mandate in order to be able to participate in the hierar-

[20] Ibid.

chical apostolate)? Pope John Paul in *Christifideles Laici* speaks of the establishment of a commission to carry out "an in-depth study of the various theological, liturgical, juridical and pastoral considerations" connected with lay ministries. It appears to have its work cut out for it.

The whole Church, not just her lay members, has a "secular dimension" that, in words of Pope Paul VI adopted by John Paul II in *Christifideles Laici,* is "inherent to her inner nature and mission".[21] As we have seen, this secular dimension of the Church and her mission received sustained attention from Vatican II, especially in its pastoral constitution on the Church in the modern world, *Gaudium et Spes.* But the idea goes back much further—as far back, for example, as the Letter to the Colossians. In one of its most cosmic formulations, it declares that the secular dimension of Jesus' mission (and therefore of the mission of the Church) concerns no less than the renewal of the entire temporal order and its restoration to the Father: "For in him [Christ] all the fullness of God was pleased to dwell, and through him to reconcile to himself all things, whether on earth or in heaven, making peace by the blood of his cross."[22]

For Christians at least, even the trivia of everyday life find, or are meant to find, a place in this scheme: "In the exercise of all their earthly activities, they can thereby gather their humane, domestic, professional, social, and technical enterprises into one vital synthesis with religious values, under whose supreme direction all things are harmonized unto God's glory."[23]

Certainly it is true, as Pope John Paul remarks, that "*all the members* of the Church are sharers in this secular dimension" of her nature and her mission, but it also is true that the

[21] Talk to Members of Secular Institutes, Feb. 2, 1972; cf. *Christifideles Laici,* 15.
[22] Col 1:19–20.
[23] *Gaudium et Spes,* 43.

laity participate in it in a way that is particularly and properly theirs.[24] Indeed, one might argue triumphalistically that the Church's real work is done mainly by laymen interacting with the secular order, while clerics occupy an ancillary position, forming and sustaining the laity much as a quartermaster corps provisions the troops who do the real fighting. Filtered through the distorting lens of extreme postconciliar counter-clericalism, such considerations may actually play a role in the identity crisis of some priests and may contribute to defections from the priesthood and to the decline in new priestly vocations. Christians are no more immune than anyone else to the pangs of frustrated self-importance.

But it is just this sort of smug portioning-out of hierarchically calibrated rankings to particular states in life and vocations that is *not* helpful at the present time—or, for that matter, at any time. The Church has suffered too much for too long from tugging and pulling for status among her members. An essential point to bear in mind about the people of the Church is the *complementarity* of all the *christifideles* and their several states in life and countless individual vocations. All are needed. All have work to do. All depend on one another.

And yet, as long as "the world" is viewed with suspicion and disparaged by the clericalist mentality, as long as clericalism encourages people to overvalue ecclesiastical structures and institutions, and as long as controlling those structures and running those institutions are treated as the privileges of a clerical (or clericalized) elite: just so long will it be more or less dishonest to tell laymen that their specific ecclesial vocation, the very expression of their dignity as Christians, points them toward the secular order. That is true, of course—it does. But to the extent that saying so masks and sustains the diehard mentality of clericalism, its repetition also cloaks and sustains an inexcusable deception.

---

[24] Cf. ibid.

How worthwhile would it be, after all, to be called to serve the world, if the world lay beyond the sphere with which Christian life is properly concerned? Someone who tells laymen their proper place is in the world while continuing to harbor this mentality is guilty of clericalist hypocrisy, skewered by one writer in pungent terms: "The more one entrusts the world to lay people, the more the church can rest under the control of the clergy."[25] There is no doubt that Vatican II's emphasis on the role of the laity in the secular order—an emphasis repeated by Paul VI, John Paul II, and others since the Council—was sincerely intended, but it will continue to generate suspicion in many people as long as clericalism persists.

The solution does not lie in adopting the reactionary postconciliar program that Maritain called "kneeling before the world". Immanentism, whether theoretical or practical, guts Christianity and the Christian vocation of meaning. It leaves Christians, both laity and clergy, incapable of rendering any distinctive service to the world and no more capable (perhaps rather less) of performing useful humanistic service than professionally competent secularists are.

The way out of this difficulty is present in the teaching of Vatican II. Pervading the whole of human history the Council perceived "a monumental struggle against the powers of darkness"; in this struggle authentic progress is possible, but so is disastrous moral failure; Christians are obliged to promote the one and resist the other. In both enterprises the distinctive Christian contribution ultimately is one and the same: "If anyone wants to know how this unhappy situation can be overcome, Christians will tell him that all human activity, constantly imperiled by man's pride and deranged by self-love, must be purified and perfected by the power of Christ's cross and resurrection. For, redeemed by Christ and made a new creature in the Holy Spirit, man is able to

[25] Parent, 155–56.

love the things themselves created by God, and ought to do so."[26] This "telling" of the gospel message is the unique service that Christ's faithful are obliged to render to the secular order: "Go into all the world and preach the gospel to the whole creation."[27] It cannot be accomplished by either kneeling to the world or shunning it.

Just as clericalism should not be perpetuated by a disparagement of the secular concealed behind the ostensibly benevolent stratagem of "entrusting" the world to laymen, so concern about overemphasizing lay ministries and clericalizing the laity should not become an excuse for imposing passivity and subservience upon them. Whether ministry does or does not belong to the laity by intrinsic right, and what effect the hierarchical validation of lay ministries may have, are not unimportant questions; but regardless of the answers, the fact is that laymen do have a duty and a right to participate actively in the institutions and programs of the Church without being subjected to clericalist domination or discrimination. Not even legitimate fear of clericalization can be allowed to obscure this.

Three areas—the liturgy, catechesis, and administration—are commonly identified as suitable for the exercise of lay ministry,[28] and these are areas of lay activity within the Church generally. Laymen working in these fields in the service of the Church will become more and more visible in the years ahead as the number of priests and religious declines. As this happens, it will be increasingly necessary to guarantee laymen employed by the Church fair treatment in regard to wages, benefits, and working conditions. But it will be even more important to ensure that these laity are not subtly victimized by a caste system in which the ultimate authority for

---

[26] *Gaudium et Spes*, 37.
[27] Mk 16:15.
[28] See *Christifideles Laici*, 23.

all the really serious decisions about the institutions and enterprises in which they work remains in the hands of clerics, even while laymen are allowed the appearance, but not the reality, of equal professional status. If this were to happen (and who doubts that it already has happened in some places?), only clericalized laymen or those unable to find jobs elsewhere would be attracted to Church-related work.

In recent years, there has been substantial progress in the treatment of the laity within the structures of the Church. Still, this remains an uneasy transitional period. Clerics, religious, and laymen have yet to work out their professional relationships in a host of Church-related programs, and their efforts to do so are hampered by a persistent clerical elitism that in many places has merely gone underground. Qualified laymen must be able to participate fully and equally in the direction of the Church-related institutions in which they work. For the laity to function with professional competence and autonomy in these institutions, it will be necessary to abandon the practice of reserving to clerics the final decisions on questions about which laymen have equal or greater competence.

Although many steps obviously remain to be taken to realize the vision of the laity and their role set out by Vatican II, the Synod of 1987, and *Christifideles Laici*, the principal need now, as I remarked earlier, is not new programs and projects but attitudinal change: change in the way we think about things.

In the United States at least, the Catholic Church already has quite enough programs and projects. In fact, the programs and projects of the Church's activist bureaucracy sometimes threaten to choke the life out of the Church. In these circumstances, there is no reason to set up a parallel network of new bureaucratic institutions committed to waging a paper war on clericalism.

Nevertheless, this general rule has one partial exception—an exception of crucial importance, since on it depends the changing of minds and hearts required finally to overcome clericalism and its offshoots. It concerns the formation of the laity.

Comprehensive programs of formation for laymen, along the lines sketched out in *Christifideles Laici,* are urgently needed.[29] Even here, though, the need—at least in the context of American Catholicism—is not so much for *new* programs as it is for intelligent use of what already exists. The Church in this country is richly blessed (and also, to some extent, heavily burdened) by a vast network of formational institutions and programs of all kinds, from Catholic universities to Sunday homilies. Instead of duplicating these with parallel structures for lay formation, we ought simply to put what we already have to better use.

The new emphasis on lay formation must focus upon spirituality and apostolate, since the two things are inseparable. There is a great need for sensitive, nonmanipulative guidance concerning the process of vocational discernment. Laymen must be told that there *is* such a thing as discernment and that it is a serious duty for every member of the Church; then they must be shown *how* to discern. For, as Pope John Paul points out, "the fundamental objective of the formation of the lay faithful is an ever-clearer discovery of one's vocation and the ever-greater willingness to live it so as to fulfill one's mission."[30]

It is imperative that the new emphasis on lay formation take seriously Vatican II's universal call to holiness. No doubt millions of ordinary laymen have quietly become great saints during the centuries of clericalism, but the elitist mentality of clericalism has created a host of disincentives to discourage the laity from aspiring to the fullness of Christian life and the perfection of charity.

---

[29] Cf. ibid., 57–63.   [30] Ibid., 58.

That is why appeals for the canonization of more laymen deserve to be heeded. The issue is not giving a boost to the status of the laity; it is that canonization is, or at least has the potential of being, an important tool of formation. This is the Church's way of calling attention to those who have lived the Christian life in a heroically exemplary manner. But not only is it important that more laymen be canonized—they need to be "ordinary" people: individuals whose lives in their exterior circumstances were enough like ours so that the rest of us might be moved to say, "With God's help, *I* could live like that, too."

Echoing the Council, Pope John Paul points out that laymen cannot live "parallel" lives—"on the one hand, the so-called 'spiritual' life, with its values and demands; and on the other, the so-called 'secular' life, that is, life in a family, at work, in social relationships, in the responsibilities of public life and in culture." Rather, all these spheres of a layman's life and activity must be integrated by the constant effort faithfully to fulfill his individual vocation; the laity are meant to enter into "the plan of God who desires that these very areas be the 'places in time' where the love of Christ is revealed and realized for both the glory of the Father and the service of others".[31]

In particular, that requires addressing the question of work and the place it should occupy in the interior lives of laymen when it is understood in its cocreative and coredemptive aspects. Shaking off the clinging grasp of the monastic-clericalist mentality, which denigrates the world and human activity in the world while at the same time avoiding secularism and immanentism, which are incapable of finding any more meaning in life than men themselves choose to give it, we need to expand, adapt, and apply the "elements of a spirituality of work" proposed, for example, by John Paul in *Laborem Exercens*.[32] A spirituality of work is essential for laymen to

[31] Ibid., 59.   [32] See *Laborem Exercens*, 25, 27.

find the means of realizing the sanctifying potential of their lives as they actually live them: "Sanctity, for the vast majority . . . implies sanctifying their work, sanctifying themselves in it, and sanctifying others through it."[33]

And what of priests?

Alongside the question of celibacy and the pros and cons of ordaining married men, the underlying issues in the so-called identity crisis of the clergy need to be brought to the surface and resolved. The confusion over roles and relationships expressed in clericalism and neocongregationalism will never be finally dispelled until priests clearly and truly understand who they are and are at peace with this identity.

The effort must begin by recognizing that the Council of Trent did not settle—in fact, did not consider—all the fundamental questions about ministry that Luther and the Protestant reformers raised: "These problems were themselves . . . the consequences of grave deficiencies in the theology of the priestly ministry and in its concrete exercise during many centuries. [They] were not . . . moreover tackled at their roots by the Council of Trent. They were adjourned and underestimated rather than truly overcome and solved."[34] These problems have remained unresolved up to the present day. As much as anything, that accounts for the persistence of clericalism, the emergence of radical counterclericalism, and the blurring of roles and relationships that weakens the Church today.

The priesthood of all the faithful, affirmed by both Protestant reformers and Pope John Paul II, is a profound reality of which, even today, many Catholic laymen are scarcely aware. The reform of the eucharistic liturgy that Vatican II mandated was meant to make this universal priesthood fully visible and operative in the Christian community's supreme

[33] Escrivá de Balaguer, 79.
[34] International Theological Commission, "The Priestly Ministry", in Sharkey, 13.

act of worship, the Mass. From that perspective, one of the most severe disappointments of postconciliar Catholic life up to now lies in the fact that lay "participation" in so many parishes seems mainly to mean keeping the congregation occupied and agitated, with little or no sense of being a community of persons engaged in a communal act of worship.

Just as important as the universal priesthood of the faithful, however, is the essential difference between the ordained and the nonordained ministries. Wherein does it lie? On the answer to that question depends the solution to the identity crisis of priests.

In the Catholic Tradition, the priest's distinct identity is found in the transforming "character" he receives in ordination. It results in his unique empowerment to act *in persona Christi,* centered above all in the Eucharist and hence also in certain other sacraments, together with the service that the priest renders by proclaiming the word (preaching-teaching-catechesis) and forming and holding together a community of Faith fitted to celebrate the Eucharist, especially through a ministry of sacramental (and nonsacramental) penance. Viewed in comprehensive and realistic terms, this is as challenging a role as any contemporary critic of a merely cultic priesthood could ask.

It also helps to situate the priest within the universal call to holiness while marking out his particular place in this context: "Truly, seeking to identify with Christ is a duty of all the faithful, because all of Christian life consists in this. However, in the case of the priest, this task assumes a decisive importance since it is closely connected to the priestly identity itself. Assuming his true identity, the priest will become an effective instrument of the one Mediator between God and man when he becomes Christ's presence and transparency."[35] In other words, while the priest is no more called to holiness

---

[35] Pope John Paul II, Address to Priests of Brazil, Oct. 13, 1991, *L'Osservatore Romano,* Eng. ed., Oct. 21, 1991.

than any other Christian, he does have a special *reason* to try to be holy: neglect of this obligation will inevitably interfere with his priestly work of making Christ present and effective.

When our thinking about the respective identities and roles of laity and priests has been clarified along the lines suggested here, we shall finally have in hand the means of shaping an authentically collaborative relationship between them in carrying on the Church's mission. Within this relationship there will be no clericalizing of the laity or "laicizing" of the clergy. The distinctive, complementary tasks of both will be recognized and appreciated, as will the absolute need that each has for the other. For the Church without lay *christifideles* would be pointless, while the Church without clerical *christifideles* would be deprived of Jesus' continuous active presence and so would cease to exist.

Finally, then, the goal of all those concerned with the problem of clericalism must be a Church in which, in the words of an author with whom I frequently have differed in these pages, "there are no longer any clerics or lay people".[36] Of course, I purposely exaggerate to make a point. Let me explain.

Entrenched resistance, much of it unconscious, exists today among clergy and laity alike to changes as radical as these words suggest. That is only to be expected. For the clericalist mind-set is not reducible to a single, simple concept and is deeply intertwined in our consciousness with the word "cleric"—and legitimate as that may be as a term referring to the proper canonical state of the priest, that state itself must be divested of the clericalist burdens it now carries, which only obscure the priest's real role in the Church, so that the laity in turn can play their role. But even though

---

[36] Parent, 198.

Catholics by and large may not be happy about the tribulations inflicted on them and their Church by clericalism and the extreme reactions against it, they have been conditioned to take this unhealthy situation for granted—to regard it as the way things *have* to be. People often would rather suffer pain to which they have grown accustomed than do what must be done to remove it.

But in this case—why not remove it? Clericalism and its offshoots offer few advantages, and these few are fast disappearing; the disadvantages, to the Church and all her members, grow increasingly burdensome. Why not put aside the clericalist mind-set once and for all and set about building a Church in which there no longer are clerics and laymen as those words are so often understood—with their subtle clericalist overtones?

Of course, if we do, we shall have to be clear about what the words mean.

A Church without clerics and laymen will *not* embrace the neocongregationalist view that ignores the essential difference between ordained and nonordained *christifideles*. Such reductionism betrays our Tradition and can only deepen our confusion. It is not the future. It is a dead end leading nowhere.

A Church without clerics and laymen *will* be one in which priests have stopped being clerics and laymen have stopped being laity as the clericalist mentality understands both: ruler and subject, superior and inferior, active agent and passive recipient, uneasy coconspirators in preserving a caste system that violates the Church's identity as *communio* and Body of Christ, tortured antagonists in an ecclesiastical power struggle carried on at the expense of the Church's mission.

A Church without clerics and laymen means many positive things.

It means a clear-eyed appreciation of the common priesthood and the common Christian vocation arising from baptism and confirmation.

It means a true understanding of what is distinctive about and proper to ordained ministry on the one hand and the lay state on the other.

It means discovering anew a priesthood whose role is truly priestly and, with it, priests who find their identity in the heart of their vocation instead of in the trappings of power, whether these be of an obvious, external sort or derive from overstepping the limits a genuinely and exclusively priestly service implies.

It means rediscovering a laity whose role is truly lay and, with it, laymen who find their identity in the heart of their vocation in the world—a vocation that stands in need, even desperately so, of the priestly service that unites laymen with their priests while enabling them to fulfill their grand vocation in the world.

It means experiencing the Church as a community of Faith with a hierarchical structure, all of whose members have complementary roles necessary to the carrying-out of her mission and to the full realization of the meaning of "Church".

It means simultaneously understanding the Church as a community of radical unity and equality—accepting the simple truth of what Paul says: among the baptized "there is neither Jew nor Greek, there is neither slave nor free, there is neither male nor female; for you are all one in Christ Jesus."[37]

It means laity and priests together facing with a divine optimism the immense challenge of leavening the entire world with the gospel, in the realization that, when they embrace their respective, distinctive, and unique roles in unity, they are embarked upon a truly God-given adventure.

It means shaping and living one's life in light of the fact that individual vocation is the dynamic principle guiding everything that a member of the Church does: the sum total of what God calls each to do, in collaboration with the others, in helping to carry on the Church's mission for the salvation

---

[37] Gal 3:28.

of the world. This requires continuing efforts to discern and accept one's vocation and live out its duties, indifferent to questions of power, prestige, status, and caste, in the conviction that the most important role anyone can play in God's providential plan is precisely that unique and unrepeatable role—humble or exalted in the eyes of others, as the case may be—that God intends for him.

When all this, and more, has become reality, no doubt we shall continue to call one another priests and laymen: there are good reasons why we should. But the words will not imply what they mean in the vocabulary of clericalism: active and passive, those who command and those who (perhaps) obey. In fact, when all this and more is reality, shall we not be able to say, in a sense embracing all that faith believes concerning ordained priesthood, baptismal priesthood, and the distinction as well as the complementarity between the two, that the primordial reality of membership in the Church—of engrafting into Christ—is not that one is a cleric or a religious or a layman, but that we are all *christifideles,* Christ's faithful, whom God calls, individually and uniquely, to work together in harmony for his kingdom's coming in this life and together to enjoy forever the definitive fulfillment of that kingdom in the next?

www.ingramcontent.com/pod-product-compliance
Lightning Source LLC
Chambersburg PA
CBHW062039220426
43662CB00010B/1574